TALK MONEY TO ME

TALK
MONEY
TO ME

THE 8 ESSENTIAL FINANCIAL
QUESTIONS TO DISCUSS
WITH YOUR PARTNER

JASON TARTICK

HARPERCOLLINS
LEADERSHIP

AN IMPRINT OF HARPERCOLLINS

Published by HarperCollins Leadership, an imprint of HarperCollins Focus LLC.

Any internet addresses, phone numbers, or company or product information printed in this book are offered as a resource and are not intended in any way to be or to imply an endorsement by HarperCollins Leadership, nor does HarperCollins Leadership vouch for the existence, content, or services of these sites, phone numbers, companies, or products beyond the life of this book.

Book design by Aubrey Khan, Neuwirth & Associates, Inc.

ISBN 978-1-4002-2691-7 (eBook)
ISBN 978-1-4002-2690-0 (HC)

Library of Congress Control Number: 2023947564

Printed in the United States of America
24 25 26 27 28 LBC 5 4 3 2 1

For Grandpa Lenny,

At the age of sixteen, you sat me down and opened up your portfolio to teach me the importance of investing and financial transparency. I will forever be grateful for you and your guidance. You are sorely missed. We love you.

For Momma Caluch & Gar-Bone,

Thank you for teaching me the value of a dollar from day one until today. Love you both dearly.

CONTENTS

1

WE WERE NOT TAUGHT

Love and Money

I knew it was bad news.

Not the disorienting, game-changing kind that leaves a seismic shift in its wake—that was a fun surprise for later—but bad enough to transform an otherwise awesome day into a raging shitstorm of chaos.

Two words. One text.

"Call me."

The sender? My boss.

It was 11:26 a.m. on April 12, 2019, when the message pinged across my phone. It was a Friday, and I had taken the day off work so I could have a three-day weekend to meet my girlfriend at the time in Las Vegas. He knew this. Which made the text all the more concerning.

Pacing the length of my hotel room, I called him. He answered on the first ring.

Fuck.

"Have you googled yourself today?" he asked. The second the words escaped his lips, my insides twisted like a coil, hell-bent on obliterating every ounce of whatever mindless liquid courage–induced euphoria Vegas injects into your veins upon arrival.

I paused and played it cool. "No . . . why?"

That was bullshit. I knew exactly why. My phone had been blowing up the past twenty-four hours with emails and texts from family members over the latest headline making its way through the tabloids.

"Why don't you google yourself and give me a call back."

The line went dead. My heart pounded. I didn't need to google anything. I already knew what was on the other end of that search.

A couple weeks earlier, my girlfriend at the time and I were doing her live podcast in New York City at the City Winery.

One of the cool things about her podcast is the confessions segment. On the surface, the goal is to laugh your ass off at various anecdotes of absurdity filled with revelations and red faces. A showcase of screwups and cringe-worthy stories that come with a mix of humiliation and hilarity that listeners can't get enough of. But if I take it one step deeper and five jumps closer to the professionally polished answer, I'd say the segment "showcases vulnerability through authentic empowerment." Essentially, it doesn't matter who you are or what you come from, we're all human, and we all have relatable, embarrassing missteps. Sharing them helps us empathize with one another while celebrating resilience. A toast to authenticity, if you will.

And fun is exactly what we were having, drinking and feeding off the crowd's energy. She jumped to her confessions segment and gave a classic story discussing the first time we hooked up. I'll be honest, I didn't see that one coming, but it certainly had the crowd laughing, me included. The next day I didn't think twice about it. Little did I know the tidal wave that would soon be heading my way. Remember that disorienting, game-changing, seismic shift I mentioned earlier? Yeah, well, that fucker was swelling to gargantuan levels. And fast. As soon as the podcast was released, the media ate it up. When the story hit the headlines, it cleaned my clock and completely swept me off my feet. A lotta people in my life were bothered by it—my parents, my grandparents. My buddies had a field day busting my chops, and apparently my family received a similar round of good-natured ribbing from their friends . . .

Last but not least came my employer. Having just come off season 14 of *The Bachelorette,* a glossy modern-day Colosseum for the love hungry, I was still new to the whole strangers-caring-or-paying-attention thing. Trying to navigate the world of media with my day job as a corporate banker intact was certainly a different kind of challenge. If there was a how-to book for corporate cogs straddling the divide between nine-to-five and frenzied public interest, my copy got lost in the mail. The headline in *People* magazine read:

"'The Bachelors' Kaitlyn Bristowe Reveals Her First Hookup with Jason Tartick Was 'Hot and Heavy.'"

I immediately called my older brother, Steven. My brother has an ownership stake in a full service marketing agency, which to me meant he definitely had experience with hiring and firing employees. I explained my predicament and asked for his advice. For a beat he was perplexed but then quickly thought to connect me with one of his friends. Turns out this friend was one of the best employment attorneys in New York City. Thank you, Steven! The lawyer advised that my employer could fire me (they could fire me at-will for anything), but he didn't think that would be in their best interest given my work performance, history with the company, and reason for potential termination. After some back-and-forth, the attorney armored me with the details I needed to know regarding next steps with my employer.

I called my boss back. "I googled myself and saw what you're referring to." Then I stopped talking, because sometimes silence creates conversation.

I knew he, too, felt uncomfortable. Maybe he wasn't happy; maybe he felt bad—he was a great guy and all. That bit of the bad news was obvious from his delay. What came next was the real gut punch.

"The bank is expecting you to resign today."

A deep breath and sigh of relief came after he delivered that message. The line went quiet.

It's funny. Even when you think something might happen, even when you're damn near certain that shit-train is on its way, the moment it becomes actuality, the second you hear the words out loud, it's a whole different beast.

Reflecting back on the conversation with the attorney, I quickly gathered my thoughts and said, "No, I'm not going to resign. If you need to fire me, you can fire me, but I won't be volunteering to resign for something that didn't come out of my mouth, especially after all I've given this company."

To his credit, I could tell he was trying to have my back: "Let me have some conversations and I'll be in touch."

For nine-plus years, I was a corporate drone. When the bank said "Jump!" I asked "How high?" I spent my entire twenties obsessing over quotas, profitability, growth, networking, and climbing the ladder. I moved thousands of miles away from my family, friends, and everything I love for this j-o-b. And just like that, after one story shared in a funny manner that was strictly meant to create entertainment and connection, the only career I had ever known was nanoseconds from imploding.

A couple hours later, my boss called me back. "You're not being fired today, but on Monday morning, the head of commercial banking and the head of human resources for the bank are flying into the Seattle office. You're expected to have a meeting with them first thing."

I tried my best to enjoy the weekend, but my family's frustration and the thought of Monday's meeting hung over me like a dark cloud. I put together a file of all my accomplishments and extracurriculars I did for the bank. It wasn't exactly the carefree hijinks I had in mind while spending three days in everyone's favorite neon-lit playground, but it felt like the right thing to do. When

Monday morning rolled around, I marched into the conference room, armored up in a suit and tie, and sat down with it all, prepared for battle. The president of commercial banking and the human resources director sat across from me.

"Disregard everything that your boss told you. We're not expecting you to resign, and we're not upset."

Two sentences into the meeting and I felt like I could exhale for the first time in seventy-two hours. The relief was short lived.

"The way we see it, you have two options: You can either eliminate media, social media, and podcasts from your life and just focus on banking. Or you can restart your career and do all the media things you want, and we'll part ways amicably."

Well, shit, I thought.

The game-changing, seismic shift was upon us.

And since you're reading this book, it should come as no surprise that I went with option two.

At that point, my girlfriend at the time and I had been dating for only a few months. Even this period of our relationship was a real crossroads. The situation created a bit of a rift just four months into dating. My family was worried, I was unemployed, and she felt somewhat responsible.

We powered and pushed through the setback together. Through that we knew if we wanted a future together, we had to take this more seriously and discuss moving in together. Over the next couple weeks we talked about our future and decided it would be best for our relationship if we moved in together. Coast-to-coast travel every weekend or so was taking a toll. We'd been doing the long-distance for several months, with her living in Nashville and me being in the Pacific Northwest. If we wanted to give our relationship a fair shot, we knew one of us would have to move. We went back and forth between Seattle and Nashville, weighing the pros and cons, ultimately settling on the Music City. She already owned a home right here, and by June, after only six months of dating, I was moving into her house. Anytime you move, whether you're living with a significant other or not, you always question yourself.

Am I making the right decision? Will this be good or bad? Is it too soon? If it turns for the worse, where would I go?

In hindsight, I wouldn't have changed my decision, but I should have stopped and questioned myself a little further. With the chaotic year of learning how to navigate the Wild West of reality TV and social media just behind me, the excitement of my new romance, and the gut punch of the unexpected loss of my job, I neglected to look at life's balance sheet. Prior to June 2019, before we moved in together, we never had a candid conversation about money. I never told her the important numbers that defined my financial health, and she didn't tell me hers. Hell, I didn't even ask. I did everything I criticize and teach not to do now—I made financial assumptions and avoided talking money! At move-in time we didn't have transparency on each other's financial status, and we didn't have a plan for our financial future together. We were caught up in love and life, which is easy to do, especially when you're going full steam ahead at two hundred miles per hour!

Now this changed throughout the years of our relationship, but to paint you a picture of how uninformed we were, here is a detailed list of all the numbers we didn't know before moving in together:

- Credit score: I didn't know hers; she didn't know mine.
- Total income: A guessing game for both of us.
- Total debt: A real his-and-her mystery.
- Annual spending habits: We never discussed it and of course didn't put together a budget.
- How bills would be split: Zero plan in place.
- Joint account: Wasn't a conversation and wasn't implemented until years after the move.
- Purchased a joint living asset without a contract: Hello, Ramen 🐾 ♥

- Four months later, purchased *another* living asset without a contract: Love you, Pinot 🐾 ♥
- Investment portfolio: I didn't know hers, she didn't know mine, and we didn't discuss if we'd open an account together, or if we would use a financial adviser.
- Net worth: Although wildly incorrect information, Google has more info on us than conversations we had with each other about it.
- Retirement goals: I had no clue when she wanted to retire and vice versa.

Holy shit, right? I'm thirty years old and for the first time in my adult life I'm unemployed, essentially homeless, moving into my new girlfriend's house across the country—2,389 miles away from my current residence to a city I know next to nothing about. And the cherry on top: I'm moving into the house that she rented with her ex and later purchased outright herself. All the while, we still hadn't had these basic conversations about money. If I could go back in time, I would shake myself by the shoulders and yell, *"Wake the hell up from the love clouds, Jason!* These conversations are mandatory!"

Here I am, someone who was taught the basic principles of money management and investing by my Grandpa Lenny at age sixteen, who went on to earn an MBA in accounting and finance, working with top CFOs, CPAs, attorneys, private equity firms, who has executed over $150 million in lending to companies in my role as a banker. I knew all the questions to ask to put us in a better position to win as one. I knew the importance of financial transparency, especially in a relationship. And I *still* made these mistakes. I tell you all of this because if I missed these material conversations, I imagine I am not alone. We can learn from mistakes I made.

There are so many what-ifs that we left ourselves open to without information.

- What was my backup plan if after a week of moving in we break up and I end up homeless and jobless?
- What if one of us, or both of us, is being crushed by debt? Tax liens, burdens, lawsuits, anything?
- What if our spending, saving, and investing habits don't align?
- What if we disagree on how to manage individual or joint expenses?

If we sat down and talked about our finances, fears, goals, and expectations, it would have saved us a lot of time, effort, and challenges. We would have gained so much more clarity to move forward as a couple. Instead, there were a few speed bumps along the way as we put systems, rules, and a joint account into place. All the things that, when not discussed, can create conflict, confusion, and misunderstanding, endangering your relationship.

LOVE ISN'T A POKER GAME

Love isn't a poker game. Aside from my relationship history but through my research it is critical to know going into this book that keeping your cards close to the vest, or worse, bluffing about your finances, is a surefire way to lose the trust and respect of the love of your life. Every game played and piece of information held back is like a small leak in a ship; enough leaks and the ship will sink. Part of being a team is knowing your partner's strengths, weaknesses, and blind spots. You can't win the game of life without sharing those vulnerabilities with each other. I wish we would've talked money and opened up about our finances sooner!

We think by ignoring the "money talk" we'll never have to face it. And that's because the likelihood is that we have been receiving those messages forever. In thirteen years of education from K–12, I was never taught about money. There wasn't a class or test I had to take on debt or personal finance, and I didn't really understand my first student loan. For shit sake, I started off majoring in history at a private school in which one year of tuition was more than the three years combined at the public college I transferred to. The truth is, the majority of us weren't taught the subject matter; but better yet we weren't even *taught how to* start the conversation. And when you don't have these conversations, you increase the likelihood of falling flat on your face. When it comes to talking about money with our significant other, too many of us shy away and bury our heads in the sand. Maybe it's because we're afraid of being judged, taken advantage of, or maybe we simply don't know how to broach the subject. In my eyes, we need to approach talking about money with our partner the same way we talk about past relationships, traumas, ambitions, and dreams. Money isn't everything, but how you approach it with your partner is. I learned from this mistake, and over the course of our relationship, we put new habits in place to avoid financial ambiguity.

The inspiration for this book is built on my mistakes, the things I wish I knew years ago, and the practices I've put in place along the way. The theories derived from my missteps and the evidence of these strategies are backed by piles of research. We're going to walk through all the numbers you can't ignore, about yourself and your partner. More importantly, I will teach you how to have conversations in a healthy and nonweaponizing way. You'll discover how to have conversations with your partner to get the same answers, helping prepare your financial future together. And if you're not in a relationship, you'll be able to answer the questions you need to know about your finances in a really digestible way so you can do some self-assessment.

BOTOX YOUR FINANCES

Talking about money can be boring. Understanding dense subject matter clicks for me when there are metaphors involved. The most effective ones are catchy, relatable, and easy to remember. I spliced metaphors throughout this book in hopes the education behind the money talk becomes more tangible for you. Botox your finances is the first one: everyone is big on the Botox thing—me included. I actually go twice a year. Why? Because it prevents wrinkles in my forehead. Think of this book as Botox for your finances. You'll have all the preventive tools you need so when you do find your person, you'll be confident and know exactly how to handle the money talk. No wrinkles required!

A quick disclaimer—this book is not *just* about getting rich, getting out of debt, or making money on your money. It's about learning how to talk money with your partner. I'll teach you the eight numbers you need to discuss with your partner, so you can live a happy life, as a couple, free of financial stress. This idea started with my Grandpa Lenny, whom I mentioned earlier. He's the one who showed me our family's investment portfolio, taught me the value of a dollar, and explained to me the importance of saving when I was just a kid. Unfortunately, Grandpa Lenny passed away on July 2, 2022. His passion for financial wellness trickled down to me and inspired me to share it with you. I'll always remember the toast he would give at family gatherings: "To health, wealth, happiness, and all the time in the world to enjoy." My hope for you and your partner is that you lead a healthy, wealthy, and happy life with time and resources to enjoy it as opposed to time wasted by worrying or arguing about your financial future. What's the point of wealth if you don't have health, happiness, and time to enjoy it all with your loved ones? So if you're ready to start your love and money journey, raise a glass and buckle up for one of the most important rides of your life! Cheers!

Dale Tartick, Jason's mother,
with Len Gross, Jason's grandfather

Ladies and gents, Dr. Leonard Gross

Grandpa Lenny and Jason sharing a laugh
after talking about the markets

Grandpa Lenny and his wife, Liz, seeing Jason's book
The Restart Roadmap for the first time

2

PEOPLE POSE, CONTEXT CHANGES, STORIES SHIFT . . .

But Numbers Don't Lie

I had the opportunity to interview former FBI hostage negotiator Chris Voss. We'll dive into his expertise and recommendations for avoiding abusive leverage in relationships in chapter 6, but here's a little taste of our conversation. From Voss, I learned the smallest tactics, from rephrasing a question to recognizing the speed at which someone talks, that can help you identify someone trying to deceive you. And when someone is trying to deceive you, the context of the narrative changes and the person's story can shift. Chris Voss even has gone as far to explain it as such: "Pay attention to your delivery. If you find yourself arguing or explaining, you're losing. If you find yourself complaining, you're losing. Conversely, if you don't make it about yourself—if you demonstrate understanding, you're winning." While words can take on many different meanings depending on the delivery, there's one thing that's consistent. You can't change the tone, context, or story of a number. Because credible numbers don't lie.

But here's the thing—we're not talking about our numbers! Only 56 percent of married and cohabiting Americans feel very comfortable talking to their partner about finances.[1] So where does this leave the other 44 percent? Are they just ignoring the topic and wishing on a star that the financial side of their relationship works itself out? Or does every conversation about money turn into some blow-up fight? Either way, this group struggles to communicate about money. And when we lack healthy communication, our relationship suffers, particularly as it relates to finances.

Why is talking about money so damn hard? It can feel like you're parading across a stage, ass out, au naturel in some humiliating fiscal fashion show. Every pore and wasted penny exposed to the masses to be shamed, blamed, and judged. I get it. You're not alone. As children, we're taught to never talk about money, for fear we might come across as rude, and our society has largely obeyed this taboo. As a result, we've developed this toxic relationship with cash. One that revolves around shame, embarrassment, or sometimes, an overinflated ego. It's no wonder that we act like a deer in the headlights when the topic comes up!

Finances trip up relationships more than almost any other factor. Nearly 73 percent of married or cohabiting Americans say monetary decisions are a source of tension in their relationship.[2] Of this group, half admit this tension has affected their intimacy with their partner. That stress can simultaneously ruin your relationship and your bank account. So why risk it? If you take time to discuss your money compatibility and goals with your partner, you'll be paying yourself **dividends** in the future. (And if you don't know the meaning of dividends . . . flip to the glossary in the back of the book for a no-BS definition! I'll do this for any finance-heavy terms you see in bold throughout the book.) Your relationship will be stronger, and likely, your joint financial status will be healthier. But as of now, the majority of couples are ignoring the problem.

The reality is, seven in ten Americans living with a partner or spouse have had a disagreement about finances in the past year. Here is a breakdown of the top five arguments:

- 36 percent argue over needs versus wants.
- 28 percent argue over spending priorities.
- 22 percent argue over large purchases without discussing them first.
- 21 percent argue over paying off debt.
- 19 percent argue over saving.[3]

Have you ever been in a disagreement like this with a significant other of yours? Or have you experienced your parents having disagreements like this? Do you want to prevent these arguments in the future? If so, the solution boils down to one key factor—communication. You might be thinking to yourself, *Duh, Jason, that's obvious!* You're right! The answer is simple, but through my research, I've found couples struggle with the execution. Many people don't know how to get the conversation started or what questions to ask. In this book I'll give you the tools to achieve both. Let me show you how to break the ice and get the convo rolling.

On my season of *The Bachelorette*, there were thirty jacked, *GQ* model–looking dudes vying for the attention of our bachelorette, Becca Kufrin. Dating is tough enough already, but being filmed on a tight schedule with a room full of overly chiseled guys who also are dating your girlfriend is like putting your relationship in a pressure cooker. The whole courting process is accelerated to the nth degree. There are group dates, producer interviews, cocktail hours, international travel, hometown dates. Personalities are twisted and stretched like saltwater taffy while you stand there in whatever shirt best accentuates your biceps as you're poked and prodded day in and day out in search of the soft spots, the raw nerves, the unhealed wounds all on the altar of ratings. If you're lucky, a few minutes might slip by where you forget your every move is being dragged through the wasteland of public scrutiny; but those moments, blissful as they may be, are about as rare as a cat's bark.

Because my one-on-one time with Becca was so finite, before each date, I would prepare by writing out questions and topics I wanted to discuss. I poured all my energy into preparing for the date. In the short period we were together, I wanted us to gather all the knowledge we could about each other because the relationship was under such a time constraint. And it was a good thing we did, because we didn't end up being each other's person, and that's okay! It's better to find out sooner rather than later.

And this wasn't just a strategy I employed when preparing for dates that would be broadcasted to millions. No, this tried-and-true tactic and I went way back. I remember being in seventh grade and having my first real girlfriend, Amie. A time when phones were still leashed to walls (I know, I'm old AF). I'd squirrel up in my dad's office, where no one could hear me, close the door, and take a blank sheet of paper from his printer. I'd jot down ideas for all the riveting conversations two twelve-year-olds could possibly have and give Amie a call. By no means was I the town Casanova, but writing out my questions helped me stay focused, preventing me from rambling on about *NFL Blitz, Super Smash Bros,* or the Buffalo Sabres. It always gave me a better idea of what I wanted to make sure I learned or shared. Weirdly enough, I still do the same thing for podcast interviews and most meetings.

You can judge my way of preparing for meaningful conversations. I get it! But I can say with confidence it's likely you will need to prepare for the money talk with your partner, and writing down your thoughts and questions will help you crystallize your intentions, fears, and expectations. I know it did for me. If the idea of talking about money is foreign to you, don't worry. I'm going to help you get warmed up to the idea. These are some fun, light questions that you can ask your partner tonight at dinner, when you're grabbing coffee, or at happy hour. Think of these questions as the appetizer. They're getting you prepped for the more serious, entrée-style conversations about money, the deeper, harder conversations that will come in later chapters. And before you ask these questions to your significant other, first reflect on your answers. How would you respond? Most importantly, these are the easy questions that will allow you to start Talking Money, while being able to identify more about you and your loved one's relationship with money.

TOP TEN TALK MONEY TO ME QUESTIONS

1. What is one thing you spend too much money on but wouldn't be willing to give up unless you were completely broke?
2. If you had to describe your relationship to finances using three words, what would they be?
3. What is your number one strength when it comes to managing your money?
4. What is your biggest weakness when it comes to managing money?
5. If you won a million dollars today (after taxes) and had to spend it all, what would you buy and why?
6. What is one thing money related, good or bad, that you learned from your parents growing up?
7. What's the most outrageous purchase you've ever made?
8. Based on that purchase, what are your feelings about it today?
9. How much do you want to earn annually? In five years? In ten years? In twenty years?
10. If you had to define when enough money is enough, how would you define that today?

Not too painful, right? They're lighthearted, could lead to some fun anecdotes, and most importantly, they'll help you dip your toes in the money conversation. No one's asking you to come in swinging hot with a heavy hitter like "How much do you make monthly?" All you need is an icebreaker to start the conversation and get the wheels turning. These are the questions that will allow you to create space so you can have discussions about money. But before diving headfirst into the topic, it's important to establish a certain level of trust and safety.

CIRCLE OF TRUST

Many of you may know this already, but I'm a big therapy guy. Since starting therapy a handful of years ago, everything in my life has gotten better. One of the things I learned from my therapist is the Circle of Trust (see figure 1).[4] Imagine a dartboard. You've seen one before. Smack dab in the center, you've got the bull's-eye. These are the people you have the deepest connections with. Your ride-or-dies, the parental units, your siblings, your better half. Basically, anyone you'd trust enough to blindfold you and navigate your ass across a freeway during rush hour. As we venture farther away from the heart of the bull's-eye, your connections and trust

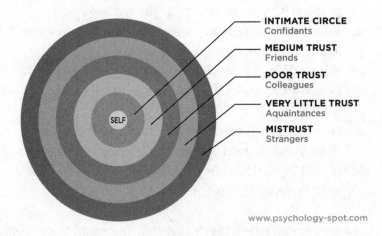

INTIMATE CIRCLE
Confidants

MEDIUM TRUST
Friends

POOR TRUST
Colleagues

VERY LITTLE TRUST
Aquaintances

MISTRUST
Strangers

SELF

www.psychology-spot.com

Figure 1

dilute. By the time you get to the fourth ring, you've got your acquaintances, or drinking buddies who are great for a few pints but wouldn't know your favorite color to save their lives. You're not baring your soul or sharing Netflix accounts with fourth-ringers. When it comes to having the money talk, I want you to exercise the same degree of caution.

While I believe financial transparency is crucial for a successful relationship, that trust should be given only to a select group of people in your life. I'm not suggesting you go on a podcast and broadcast your earnings. No one does that . . . unless I'm interviewing you on *Trading Secrets*. Rather, take stock and analyze who's in your bull's-eye. If you've already established a firm foundation of trust with this group, and there's no question about their intentions, then I encourage you to take the next step and Talk Money with them. Opening the financial floodgates will allow your little Circle of Trust to grow stronger, enable you to lean on each other for support, and will increase the likelihood of achieving your financial goals. Start here and then work these conversations to where you feel comfortable. You may even grow to the point that you'll come on my podcast and tell all your Trading Secrets!

As mentioned earlier, only half of couples feel comfortable talking about finances to their partner, so it's not unreasonable to assume that many people still haven't created that circle of trust when it comes to money, no matter how long you've been together. It's imperative we fix that. The number one reason for divorce is infidelity. The number two reason is financial, aka money fights.[5] I'm sure a friend has told you, or maybe you've told a friend, about an issue that reeks of potential infidelity or a situation that concerns you, like a flirty text or something equally eyebrow raising. Did you run to your friends for advice or comfort? I'm guessing yes.

Now flip the script to a financial fiasco; rampant spending, looming debt, income, credit. Who's in your corner? How big is your circle? And can you trust they'll deliver credible, intelligent, level-headed advice?

Ideally, your financial squad should have just as many members as your infidelity advisory board, but from the research I have done, it's likely not.

I don't know about you, but that's a pretty serious wake-up call for me. So how do we correct it? Well, once you've established a Circle of Trust and broken the ice with the Top Ten Talk Money to Me Questions, it's time to ask the hard-hitting questions. The rest of this book is structured around eight essential questions relating to your financial wellness and goals that you need to know about yourself and your partner. Once you answer, ask, and explore the meaning behind these questions, all the fear, shame, and awkwardness around love and money will evaporate.

ELITE EIGHT: ESSENTIAL NUMBERS TO KNOW AND COMMUNICATE

1. What is your credit score?
2. How many financial accounts do you have?
3. What are your annual expenses?
4. What is your expense-to-income ratio?
5. What is your debt-to-income ratio?
6. What is your net worth?
7. What is your investing risk-tolerance score?
8. What age do you want to retire?

Every chapter in this book will be a deep dive into each of these questions. The answer to every question is an objective number. I chose to approach the topic this way because numbers don't lie. If you think the question is too vague or immaterial, I promise in each chapter I will further explain the importance. The gray area can become confusing, so this book is designed so that your answer and your partner's answer should be black and white—we're eliminating the gray area. In each chapter, we'll discuss what the number means, how it can be improved, and how you can have discussions to work on your financial future as a couple. Behind each of these numbers is a story. I'll share some of my own, no matter how personal and messy they may be, plus an interview with one of the victims from Netflix's *The Tinder Swindler,* conversations in the fantasy suite with some of your favorite *Bachelor* contestants, and a shocking tale from one of *Say Yes to the Dress*'s biggest stars.

When revealing your numbers to your partner, and vice versa, practice patience, empathy, and effective listening. It's a delicate dance, and trust me, I've forgotten the moves and stepped on some toes along the way. Stepping into the money conversation is uncharted waters for many, and the worst thing either of you could do is judge or make the other person feel shame around their financial standing. So be a good partner, and listen to their story. It will benefit you both in the long run.

With all that in mind, are you ready to get started? Let's grab a hammer and start breaking down the walls we've put up! It's time to stop putting off the discussions we know we should have but have been too afraid to broach. After you're done with this book, you'll never live another day without knowing these numbers. That's a huge win. For you, for your partner, and for your relationship. If you have any questions along the way, there's a QR code for you to join my Facebook group. Fire off any questions as they come to mind, I'll answer them, and you can Talk Money to me!

3

WHAT IS YOUR CREDIT SCORE?

No One Can Gaslight with Their Credit Report

DING DING DING!!!
IT'S THE CHAPTER 3 OPENING BELL

- $ Knowing your credit score and your partner's credit score is just as important as knowing their birthday
- $ All show, no dough: financial gaslighting is a thing; eliminate it
- $ What the hell is credit anyway?
- $ Your credit report is your financial scorecard: how to pull it, understand it, and dispute it
- $ Find your credit score, know what factors affect it, and know how to improve it
- $ How to talk about credit with your significant other

Imagine it's your birthday. Naturally you're excited. There's always something magical about a birthday, no matter how old you're turning. You don't have any set plans yet, but you know you'll be spending the day with your significant other. Maybe you'll go out to a nice dinner, grab some cocktails, or if you're anything like me, hopefully you have an experience lined up, maybe travel, a concert, or even tickets to a Broadway show (who doesn't love *Hamilton*?).

But imagine this. You wake up on your special day, and when you see your significant other for the first time, it's just like any other Tuesday. Nothing bad has happened; it's simply the status quo. As the conversation unfolds, you're hit with the realization that your partner has forgotten your birthday. This isn't some random hookup from a dating app. This is your serious, long-term partner. Potentially your partner for life. And they forgot the most basic, yet most important, piece of information about you besides your freaking first and last name.

A million emotions are running through your head: shock, disappointment, and understandably, anger. So, you ask, "Did you forget it's my birthday?!" Naturally, that's when their eyes are gonna bulge, empathy is going to rush through them, and they'll begin sincerely apologizing with a reason that's probably a little frustrating but totally understandable. Except none of that happens. Instead, they just stare back at you, confused. "I didn't know today was your birthday."

And then it hits you like a ram; you're the one who messed up. How could they remember a date . . . a number . . . *you* never told them.

Obviously, this is just an exaggerated hypothetical, but that's what I want to highlight here. Numbers follow us throughout our life: the date we're born, our age, our height, our phone number, our address, the year we graduated from high school or college—the list is endless. These numbers are very open; there's no stigma or taboo around them. We share them with the people in our lives, and as we saw with the birthday example—it's really odd and quite frankly concerning if you don't!

When I moved in with my then girlfriend, we didn't know each other's credit scores. In my brain, not knowing this information is like not being aware that June 19 is her birthday and her not knowing mine is October 24. It's *that* freaking important. You might be thinking, *Whoa, Jason, that's a little dramatic.* Trust me, it's not. Unless you have a pile of cash in your mattress, a good credit score is crucial if you want to qualify to borrow money. This includes a mortgage for a house, a car loan, and credit cards.

A lower credit score means the borrower is higher risk; a higher credit score means the borrower is lower risk. In the world of interest rates, an individual with a low credit score will have a harder time getting bank loans, and they may pay thousands, maybe hundreds of thousands, or even millions of dollars more in interest over their lifetime than an individual with a high credit score, who will be charged a lower interest rate and will have easier approval processes. The higher the risk of you repaying the bank, the more expensive money becomes. The money saved by having a lower interest rate is free cash that you could use for investing, retirement, vacations, or living a more comfortable lifestyle.

When you look at your entire financial profile, the backbone is credit. It provides banks the opportunity to assess the risk they take on when they are providing you their money. And, when you marry the love of your life, you're marrying their credit score and credit report, meaning any challenges that come with their low credit score could extend to you. Which, at the time, may seem like small potatoes compared to an overbearing mother-in-law with a PhD in unsolicited advice or a rowdy uncle who sees "drunk and disorderly" as a personal challenge. But trust me, that shit will haunt you harder and longer than any nightmare in-law ever could.

This number carries a ton of weight on your ability to get credit, your access to attractive banking options, and the total cost because of higher interest rates over the entirety of your life. So, why is something that is so important in our lives—something the system intensely analyzes and then assigns to your name a numerical score, something that changes based on financial behaviors—taboo to talk about?

If this doesn't click, let me ask you a few questions:

	Yes	No
Would you ride a roller coaster without a seat belt?		
Would you dive headfirst into the shallow end of a pool?		
Would you go skydiving with an instructor who hasn't completed their required training?		
Would you bet half of your life savings on red or black at the roulette table?		
Would you get on a plane if you saw the pilot drinking?		

I'm assuming the answer to all of these questions is probably not. And that's because you're instinctively assessing the risk associated with each situation. There are primal responses we have to high-risk situations. Our natural instincts immediately kick in and scream "Caution: Danger Ahead!" telling us to put on a seat belt before riding a roller coaster or to think twice before making a life-altering decision.

Is this risk worth the reward?

The point is there's risk that we face, assess, and make decisions about every day. One of the biggest risks we can take is committing to a lifelong partner without first understanding the financial life we want together, our collective credit scores that will help dictate that life, and our historical behaviors that can be defined in our credit reports. It may be uncomfortable to bring up credit scores when you're planning your future together. Maybe you're scared it will rock the boat, or you will find out something that will change how you see your partner. The truth is, you will eventually find out. Wouldn't you like to know before you find your dream house and the bank denies your loan? Or even worse, buy a home and then realize the IRS instantly owns your home? Yes, this is real, and yes, we will share this story in chapter 4. And conversely, just because you or your partner has a terrible credit score doesn't have to mean the relationship is over. It just means you have transparency and a need to work together to build a plan that turns the score around. The plan of action is the easy part; knowing you both need to take action as one is the hard part.

WHY YOU SHOULD CARE

The next table shows the average interest rate on a thirty-year mortgage for different credit scores. The median sale price of a home in the United States as of Q1 2023 was $436,800.[1] For simplicity let's use a round number and real-life scenario: Say you and your partner want to buy a $300,000 home and you decide on a 5 percent down payment. After depositing your $15,000 down payment, your total loan from the bank is $285,000. Reasonable enough, right? Well, what if I told you the difference in interest paid for the highest credit score range of 760 to 850 compared to the lower range of 620 to 639 over a thirty-year fixed rate mortgage period is $110,626.31.

I'm going to repeat that.

For the same exact house, the individual with the lower credit score is going to pay $110,626.31 *more* than the individual with the higher credit score over a thirty-year period. If you don't believe me, do the math yourself! The reason the individual with the lower credit score is paying about 25 percent more in interest is because their credit score directly impacts the interest rate determined by the bank. It's also important to know that if your credit score is below 620, you might not qualify for a conventional loan, which is a standard mortgage offered by major commercial banks.

It should be noted that there are alternative options for obtaining a loan with a credit score of 620 or less. For example, applying for loans with US-backed government agencies like the **Federal Housing Administration (FHA)** or working with a mortgage broker to attain a nonqualified mortgage.[2] That being said, these alternatives might come at a cost, including higher interest rates or a larger down payment. If that's not a good enough reason to start caring about your credit, I'm not sure what is.

FICO Score	National Average Mortgage APR (%)	Amount Paid in Interest Over 30-Year Period ($)
620 to 639	8.068	472,711.78
640 to 659	7.522	433,940.34
660 to 679	7.092	403,951.42
680 to 699	6.878	389,214.64
700 to 759	6.701	377,123.26
760 to 850	6.479	362,085.47

Info used from: https://www.businessinsider.com/personal -finance/average-mortgage-interest-rate (as of June 2023)

Are we okay with standing by and leaving tens of thousands, or even hundreds of thousands, of dollars on the table just because the initial conversation with our partner may feel a little awkward? Research tells us the risk of starting the conversation with your partner is worth the reward of financial stability later in life. We need to normalize financial transparency. Sometimes a far-fetched statement creates urgency, and if it's me telling you that knowing your significant other's credit score is just as important as knowing their birthday, I will scream it loud and proud. Know your partner's birthday and know their credit score!

Before starting this conversation, it's important to keep in mind that we must avoid weaponizing vulnerability at all costs. If you have a low credit score, it doesn't determine your value as a human, and if you have a high credit score, it doesn't mean you're the best thing since sliced bread. It's simply a number. A barometer for your historical behaviors, but a number that can be easily improved with the right strategies, which I will discuss later in this chapter.

If you're ignoring the facts, lying to others, or hiding from your partner, you're cheating everyone. Eventually, your lies will catch up to you and will be exposed. And if your partner doesn't recognize your deception, well, your uphill battle continues, because "the system" is designed to catch liars. The risk of letting fraud slip through the cracks creates too much liability for our government and financial institutions. You may think you can scam the banks by forging your credit report or score, but in the end, your lie will be discovered. This type of credit fraud falls under Section 1029 of the US Code Title 18 and can have serious consequences.[3]

GASLIGHTING WITH YOUR CREDIT

If you've followed any therapist on social media or watched any episode of *The Bachelor*, *Vanderpump Rules*, or *Love Is Blind* in the past few years, you're bound to have heard the term *gaslighting*. To refresh your memory, it's a form of psychological abuse, typically between couples in a romantic relationship, where the abuser methodically withholds information from or provides fake information to the victim. This has the gradual effect of making the victim anxious and confused, questioning their own memory and perception of reality. This term actually comes from a 1940s movie called *Gaslight*, where the husband manipulates the wife into thinking she's insane.[4]

Pretty heavy stuff and messed up shit, right? Unfortunately, just like a partner can gaslight you on the emotional side of a relationship, gaslighting can come in the form of financial abuse too. When it comes to love and money, financial deception is more common than you may realize.

According to the most recent Financial Infidelity Survey conducted by the National Endowment for Financial Education, among couples who have ever combined finances in a current or past relationship, about 43 percent have committed financial deception.

Some examples of financial deception include hiding bills, cash, bank accounts, and purchases. Of the group that has committed financial deception, more than 85 percent said their deception has affected their current or past relationships in some way. Most of the group said that their actions caused an argument with their spouse or caused less trust in the relationship, while 16 percent said it ultimately led to divorce.[5] These stats are alarming and certainly telling.

The best way to avoid becoming another statistic is by starting to *Talk Money*! First talk about money with yourself, and once you've stepped into that, start having conversations with your partner. If you don't know where to start, let me help.

Start with Your Credit Score.

By lifting the curtain, finding your credit score, and sharing it with your significant other, you're creating a solid bond of trust. Undoubtedly, if you share your financial story, your partner will be more open to sharing theirs. It's the foundation of any healthy relationship, a give-and-take. Sometimes you're the bug; sometimes you're the windshield. Sharing your credit score and report with each other takes the deception, confusion, and gaslighting out of the money side of your relationship. The assumptions are thrown out the window. The two start connecting as one.

In our world it's not a crime to gaslight people, so be aware! Be very aware! But it becomes a crime when you gaslight and deceive financial institutions.

I think we can all agree, whether emotional or financial, gaslighting sucks. Yet the legal consequences for gaslighting people are minimal. It's your job to put your detective hat on. Always remember, people can lie, but credible numbers don't!

WHAT THE HELL IS CREDIT?

At this point we know the importance of credit and why it's so valuable to financial institutions that people will risk going to jail to make their credit look better than it is. Now let's get into what credit actually is.

Credit is an agreement bound by a contract in which a borrower receives a sum of money or something of value and repays the lender at a later date, generally with interest and fees. When a lender provides "credit" to a borrower, they are immediately taking on the big risk of not being paid back. As a result of this inherent risk, the lender will analyze the borrower in depth to determine the likelihood of being repaid in full. There is a long list of things a lender will analyze to estimate this risk of a borrower, but one's credit score is a massive factor. The credit score is a three-digit number calculated by a scoring system that summarizes an individual's creditworthiness, which is used as a guide when considering approval. If approved, one's credit score will also impact the interest rate and structure of the loan.[6]

Here's an example we can all understand: Imagine you're a kid on the playground and you have two dollars to use at the ice cream truck. Your friend comes up to you and asks to borrow one of your dollars so he can also buy a frozen treat. Being the kind kid you are, you agree, but only if your friend promises to bring you the loaned dollar tomorrow at school. He agrees, and you seal the contract with the all-holy pinky promise. Tomorrow comes, no dollar. The next day comes, no dollar. Finally, on the third day, you confront your friend and ask him for the replacement dollar. He responds in the way you dreaded, stating he doesn't have any money today, but he'll get you back later.

In this example, we have an exchange of credit, which is one dollar. We have the contract agreement binding your friend to repay the loan in the form of a pinky promise. And we have your friend's new estimated credit history, which in your eyes is low, considering there is a high risk you will never be paid back based on the current behavior of your friend. In credit analysis we refer to this as "character." Moreover, it's likely if your friend wants to borrow a dollar again, you will say no or you may even say, "The risk in lending you one dollar is high so I will lend you one dollar, but I would like two dollars in return." This, my friends, is the most basic example possible that depicts how bank lending operates.

From ice cream cones to a quick history lesson, let's talk about how credit came to be. Believe it or not, credit has been around for more than five thousand years! According to a report from Visual Capitalist and Equifax, credit is thought to have started in 3500 BC, when the first urbanized city, Sumer, was built. There are ancient texts showing the first loans were used here for the purpose of buying land. Thousands of years later, in 50 BC, the Roman philosopher Cicero wrote that his neighbor purchased 625 acres of land for 11.5 million coins. Now his neighbor didn't lug around chariots full of gold coins to pay for this land; he used credit! Cicero actually wrote in Latin *"nomina facit, negotium conficit,"* which literally means, "He uses credit to complete the purchase."[7]

Flash-forward almost two thousand years to England in the early nineteenth century, where we have the birth of modern credit. A group of tailors got together and exchanged information on customers who neglected to pay off their debts. While this is a very early record of modern credit, we see the basic concept of lenders gathering data relating to a borrower's debt history. Our current, formalized consumer credit model wasn't developed until the early twentieth century, when Henry Ford's iconic invention of the Model T made automobiles accessible to the masses. For many families back then, and even today, buying a car in cash is likely not a viable option. As a result, General Motors created the idea of financing, to allow individuals with a lack of cash flow to purchase vehicles on an installment plan.[8]

After learning about the history of car financing and the massive impact credit scores have on each of us, I was reminded of a story from my buddy PJ. PJ is a former car salesman, now finance and insurance manager, for one of the largest dealerships in the state of New York. He told me a story last year that I will never forget and must share. His dealership is unique in the sense that he has sold extremely exotic cars, from a $1.3 million Ford GT, to completely standard cars, like a Chevrolet Cobalt for $11,000. One day, a customer saunters in, suave looking dude, the kind who wears confidence like a second skin. Let's call him Mr. Sleek. My man purchases a $150,000 Mercedes G-Wagon. Luckily for him, he's got an exceptional credit score of 812.

Mr. Sleek puts zero down and receives a 2 percent interest rate for seventy-two months. His monthly car payment is $2,200, and his **insurance premium**, largely due to his history and good credit, is only $120 a month. The all-in monthly cost for the $150,000 G-Wagon comes to $2,320. Don't get me wrong, that's a ton of money, but for the man wearing swagger like cologne, the payment was only a small percentage of his income. Now here's the kicker. Contrast to later that day, when a young sprite in her mid-twenties glides in to purchase her first ever vehicle. Exciting stuff, right? Well, maybe not. Our fresh-faced buyer wasn't taught the importance of credit or how it could impact her life. As a result, over the past few years, she cosigned on multiple loans with various family members and friends because, at the time, she had good credit. The cosigned loans defaulted because the primary borrower missed some payments, which negatively impacted her credit score. Now, our young customer's score is below 600, which makes taking out a loan really expensive. She purchases a $21,000 Toyota Camry, with an interest rate of more than 20 percent. Her monthly payment is approximately $700 for seventy-two months.

Think that's bad? It gets worse. Our youthful everyday hero had never owned a car, so she didn't have speeding tickets or major accidents (a plus, right?), but because her credit score was so unfavorable, only one or two carriers would quote their auto insurance. Because of this, the insurance premium per month for this vehicle was $1,400. So this customer's car payment, including the interest, insurance, and the actual car loan, was $2,100 a month for a $21,000 vehicle. Compare that to Mr. Sleek who bought a $150,000 G-Wagon for only $200 more per month. This story is absolutely bananas! But here's the thing—the outcome could have been so different if there was more education about credit. The newbie-car-owner who cosigned on all those loans probably would have thought twice before signing the contract, thus preserving her credit score.

Reflecting on this story makes me wonder why we were never taught about personal finance and credit in school, especially considering it can significantly affect the quality of our lives, for better or worse. Credit has been around for more than five thousand years and will be around for another five thousand years. This concept is not going anywhere. Credit is a staple for financial institutions' past, present, and future business dealings. Instead of avoiding credit, we need to get our hands dirty and do the work to fully understand what the hell credit is.

In the mid-twentieth century, Bill Fair teamed up with Earl Isaac to create the Fair Isaac Corporation, with the goal of creating a standardized, objective credit scoring system. Today, that company goes by the name **FICO**. The current FICO score system debuted in the late 1980s and has become the industry standard. The FICO score ranges from 300 to 850 and is determined by five driving factors:

1. Payment history
2. Total debt owed
3. Length of your credit history
4. Total credit mix (aka different forms of credit)
5. Recent credit inquiries or new credit[9]

The three major credit bureaus, Experian, TransUnion, and Equifax, track your personal financial information to determine your credit score. They all use credit scoring models created specifically for them by the FICO. You likely have at least one credit file with one of the big credit bureaus if you've ever borrowed money. This includes everything from a credit card to a student loan, mortgage, or auto loan.

It's important to note that these three credit bureaus are government approved to provide your credit score. They are subject to the **Fair Credit Reporting Act (FCRA)**, which is a federal law that governs how credit reporting agencies handle your financial information. FCRA determines how consumers' credit information is obtained, how long it is kept, and how it is shared with others. FCRA also limits who is allowed to see your credit report and under what circumstances. In essence, FCRA is a safeguard set in place to ensure you aren't being screwed over by the three big credit bureaus.[10]

It also guarantees you certain consumer rights. For example, you have the right to verify the accuracy of your credit report when it's pulled for employment purposes, you can dispute and have any inaccurate information corrected in an effort to repair your credit, and you're entitled to receive a notification if information in the bureau's file has been used against you when applying for credit or other transactions.

Before you can have discussions about credit or a credit report with a loved one, you must know how to pull and understand your own credit report. Now that we know what credit is, the reasoning behind it, what makes up your credit score, and how you are protected, let's pull your score.

HOW TO PULL YOUR CREDIT REPORT AND SCORE

1. Go to www.AnnualCreditReport.com. This site has an awesome reputation. It's actually the official site to get your free annual credit report, which is a right guaranteed by federal law. Plus, AnnualCreditReport.com is verified

by the **Consumer Financial Protection Bureau (CFPB)**.

2. Click on the big red button on the website that says, "Request Your Free Credit Reports."

3. Fill out the form with your name, birthday, social security number, and current address.

4. If you have moved in the past two years, you will need your previous address.

5. One thing that might trip you up, at least it tripped me up, is your zip plus-four code. You probably know your zip code, but not many people know the plus-four digits off the top of their head. You can find those digits here: https://www.unitedstateszipcodes.org/.

6. After you input all of this information, hit "next" at the bottom of the screen.

7. Then you will be prompted to request your credit report. You will have the option to order credit reports from all three companies, Experian, TransUnion, and Equifax, or order one at a time. Should you order all three? Yes! They will all be free within a twelve-month period.

8. The website will then ask you a series of questions to verify your identity.

9. Here are some examples of questions they might ask:
   ○ Which of the following is a current or previous employer?
   ○ Based on our records, you opened an auto loan. Please select the dollar range for your total monthly payment.
   ○ Which of the following are the last four digits of your primary checking account number?
   ○ Which of the following is your current license plate?
   ○ What is your cell phone number? (Then they'll text a passcode to you to enter on the website to verify your identity.)

10. Once you have verified your identity, you will be taken directly to your credit report, which you can download, save, or print.

If you've never seen your credit report, you might be a little shocked. There is a ton of information. It lists every address you have ever lived at. I swear this takes up almost a full page on my report. Thank you for all the relocations, corporate America! But honestly, all of this information is good stuff.

The credit report gives you the opportunity to see your score-card and check your information to make sure it's accurate. Even though it might seem tedious, make sure your addresses are correct, your work history, your cell phone number, and most importantly, make sure all your credit balances are accurate. You're looking for anything that may be inaccurate because inaccuracies must be disputed. If you have balances or credit lines that don't correlate to you, be cautious. There's a lot of fraud out there. Fraudsters will attempt to steal your identity and open credit lines under your name, without you knowing. After a thorough look, I can report back that everything on my report looked clean and accurate.

HOW TO DISPUTE YOUR CREDIT REPORT

1. Contact the credit reporting company that made an error. The big three are Equifax, Experian, and TransUnion. You can file the dispute online, by phone, or mail.

    Equifax
    ○ Online: www.equifax.com/personal/credit-report -services/credit-dispute/
    ○ By phone: (866) 349-5191

Experian
- Online: www.experian.com/disputes/main.html
- By phone: (888) 397-3742

TransUnion
- Online: https://dispute.transunion.com
- By phone: (800) 916-8800

2. Be prepared with the following information:
   - Your personal contact information
   - An explanation of the mistake and *why* it's an error
   - Any evidence you have that supports your dispute, such as invoices, financial statements, or contracts
   - The report confirmation number from your credit report, found at the very top of your credit report

3. Request the credit reporting company either remove or correct the error.

4. Save copies of all documentation and communication with the credit report company in relation to the dispute.

5. You will also have to dispute the information with the company that provided the financial information to the credit reporting company. These agencies are called furnishers. For example, if you have an auto loan with PNC Bank, you will have to reach out directly to the bank. The easiest way to do this is via mail or email. Follow the dispute letter template on the FICO website: https://www.myfico.com/credit-education/credit -reports/fixing-errors.

The number one thing to do is to make sure the status of your credit history is accurate. The report will state the lending company, the amount of the loan, and the status of the loan. If you have late payments, this is where it will be showcased and how it's affecting your credit score. For example, it will show the condition of the loan, which is either open or closed. It will also show the pay status, which can be any of the following: pays as agreed, paid/closed never late, settled, or 30/60/120 days past due. Pays as agreed and paid/closed never late mean you're in good standing. Settled and past due status means your payment history is negatively affecting your credit score. This is extremely important as payment history makes up 35 percent of your total credit score. We'll dive deeper into this shortly.

You'll have the ability to save your credit report. I suggest you use it as a benchmark for next year. If you ordered your credit report through Experian, there will be a large purple button that prompts you to get your FICO score. According to Experian, 90 percent of lenders use your FICO score. As one of the three credit bureaus in the United States, Experian is a reputable company that has been around for more than 125 years and is backed by the FCRA. Plus, it's free and available to everyone.

HOW TO GET YOUR FICO SCORE WITH EXPERIAN

1. If you did not order the Experian credit report, go to their website directly: www.experian.com/consumer-products/credit-score.html.
2. Select the big, purple button that says, "Check your FICO score for free."
3. You'll then be taken to the registration page. You will need to input your name, address, and email. You will also be prompted to create a password.
4. Next, you will be taken to a page to verify your identity. You will need the following:
   - last four digits of your Social Security number
   - date of birth
   - phone number

5. After you verify your identity, hit "submit secure order."
   Then you will be directed to your credit score.

Mine is 796, earning me a "very good" rating.

The FICO credit scoring model uses these five factors when evaluating your credit score:

1. Payment history (35 percent): Whether you've paid past credit accounts on time
2. Amounts owed (30 percent): The total amount of credit and loans you're using compared to your total credit limit, also known as your utilization rate
3. Length of credit history (15 percent): The length of time you've had credit
4. New credit (10 percent): How often you apply for and open new accounts
5. Credit mix (10 percent): The variety of credit products you have, including credit cards, installment loans, finance company accounts, mortgage loans, and so on.

Here's a look at where I stand with these five factors:

35 percent of score Payment history	Exceptional
30 percent of score Amount of debt	Very good
15 percent of score Length of credit history	Very good
10 percent of score Amount of new credit	Good
10 percent of score Credit mix	Very good

My biggest strength is payment history. This is great considering it's the heaviest weighted factor evaluated by FICO. My weak spot is the amount of new credit. In my case, I haven't had much new credit recently. Having too many new credit cards is looked poorly upon by lenders, but not having enough new credit may also make you appear risky due to lack of history and available information. In the report, we can take a deeper dive into these score ingredients and examine exactly what actions, or inactions, are affecting my score:

Lack of recent non-mortgage loan information	Hurting
No missed payments	Helping
Low revolving credit usage	Helping
Recent credit card usage	Helping
No collection of public record	Helping

Lack of recent non-mortgage loan information: Here you can see I'm in the red when it comes to recent non-mortgage loan information. I have a zero balance when it comes to non-mortgage debt, such as student and auto loans. Believe it or not, sometimes having a zero balance is considered riskier. This is because they want to know that you make payments on time to multiple forms of outstanding credit. If you don't have payments to make, they can't know if you make them. There are multimillionaires with terrible credit scores because they pay for everything with cash. The credit bureaus do not have enough information to determine whether this person would make payments on time because they haven't had anything to make payments on. The ideal situation for a lender would be to have a borrower with a non-mortgage loan with no missed payments and a low balance. Fortunately, by the time this book is out, I will have a mortgage loan on my report and that should boost my credit!

No missed payments: When it comes to no missed payments, I promise that I practice what I preach. No missed payments on my report! The more severe, recent, and frequent your late payment information is, the more it will negatively impact your FICO score. Even if you can't pay the balance of your credit card, you have to pay the minimum. Don't miss this. Missing the minimum payment will ding your credit. Miss it by more than thirty days and that could follow you for years.

Low revolving credit usage: My credit card limit is $38,000, but I'm only using 2 percent of that total available balance every month. Keep this percentage low so you aren't biting off more than you can chew when the bill comes.

Recent credit card usage: Credit cards aren't all bad. Using a credit card responsibly can show you are less risky to lenders. Before opening a credit card account, you have to be honest about your spending discipline. Credit cards are not for everyone, and that's okay. Swiping your card blindly can make it difficult to track your spending. The money doesn't leave your account immediately; they allow you to pay only minimum balances, and the card won't get declined if you exceed the balance of your bank account, like a debit card would. If you end up forgetting payments or carrying a balance, your credit score will be worse off than if you hadn't used a credit card at all.

No collection or public record: An example of a public record is bankruptcy. According to FICO, I have no collection notice or public record associated with my name, which is looked upon favorably by lenders. If you have been through a bankruptcy, it's not the end of your financial life. Depending on what type of bankruptcy you file, it will affect your credit only for seven to ten years.

JASON'S CREDIT HOW-DO-YA-DOS!

Now that you know your credit score, you'll be fully prepared to talk credit with your loved ones, partner, or future partner. But let's review some strategies that will allow you to improve your score, while providing suggestions for when you start Talking Money with others. Unless you have a perfect score of 850, everyone can work on upgrading their credit game plan. As we saw with my score, I definitely have some room for improvement! The next table summarizes my top credit can-dos you can apply today. Easy things you can do for your credit. They are in three tiers based upon what your credit score is: red, yellow, and green. If you're in the red zone, and are considered to have a poor score, my suggestions are going to be way different than if you fall in the yellow or green zones. My credit can-dos for the yellow and green zones, or fair and good scores, are very similar. In an effort to keep these strategies straight-forward, I combined the yellow and green zones to create the "lime zone." Now that we have the limes, all we need is some salt and a shot of tequila!

Red Zone: FICO Score 350–659

Jason's Credit How-Do-Ya-Dos!	Strategy
Review credit report for errors	Make sure all employment information, address, phone number, and spelling is correct. File a dispute if anything is inaccurate or smells fishy.
Get a secured credit card	If you don't have credit history or are trying to rebuild your credit, you might find it difficult to open a standard credit card. Instead, try using a secured credit card as a stepping stone to help you build and boost your credit. You'll need to provide the credit card company a refundable security deposit as collateral to open the card. Your deposit is the equivalent of your credit limit. If you put $1,000 as your deposit, your line of credit is only good up to $1,000. That way,

Jason's Credit How-Do-Ya-Dos!	Strategy
Get a secured credit card (continued)	if you struggle to pay off your card, there's no risk to the bank because they can use your deposit as collateral. It's essentially a small step to start building trust. (See https://www.bankrate.com/finance/credit -cards/secured/#closer).
Become an authorized user or find a cosigner	If your partner, parent, or trusted friend has good credit, they can add you as an authorized user to their credit card. The authorized user now has access to use the card and can be the benefactor of the primary cardholder's good credit. This does not negatively impact the primary cardholder's credit. But if credit mistakes are made, like late payments, those actions will negatively affect both of your scores. You should keep in mind that the primary cardholder is the only individual on the hook for paying the bill at the end of the month. If adding an authorized user, make sure there is a certain level of trust. Finding a cosigner is quite similar, just with reversed roles. If you pursue this can-do, sign a joint contract that binds both of you to operate responsibly. (See https://www.creditkarma .com/credit-cards/i/add-authorized-user -credit-card).

Lime Zone (Yellow and Green): FICO Score 660–850

Jason's Credit Hack	Strategy
Decrease credit utilization	Your **credit utilization rate** is the amount of revolving credit you're using divided by your total available credit across those accounts. Lenders often like to see a credit utilization rate at or below 25 percent. Having available credit indicates that you're only using the credit that you need, as opposed to using all that you have available to you. This is to be seen as a positive sign for lenders. Here's a pro tip for keeping your credit utilization low: keep old credit card

Jason's Credit Hack	Strategy
Decrease credit utilization (continued)	accounts open. When trying to increase your score, try to avoid closing any accounts that have been paid off, even if you no longer use them. Keeping these accounts open will help maintain the length of your credit history and decrease your credit utilization rate. Here's an elite tip: this is ass-backwards, but you could also request an increase in your credit limits and then *not* use the additional credit available. That, too, would decrease your utilization rate. Only do this if you will *not* be tempted to use the additional credit available.
Set your bills on autopay	Set up all of your bills like utilities, subscriptions, car payment, mortgage, and credit card on automatic payments. When implementing this feature, make sure you're paying the full statement balance, not the minimum balance. This will help decrease the amount you pay in interest over time, while simultaneously decreasing your credit utilization rate. Make sure you're actively watching balances so that you don't overdraw your bank accounts.
Credit mix	Have at least one installment loan and one line of revolving credit. An installment loan is a close-ended credit account that you pay back over a set period of time, for example, a mortgage, personal loan, or auto loan. An example of revolving credit is a secured credit card or a standard credit card. When I wrote this book, I didn't have an installment loan, and as we saw, this negatively affected my FICO score. As you read this book right now, I've taken my own advice and added an installment loan as a strategy to help improve my score.

WHERE DO YOU STAND?

So now that you have your credit score, you're probably pretty curious to see how your score compares to others. According to a study conducted in 2023 by MoneyGeek, the average FICO credit score for consumers in the United States is 711.[11] Based on the results of your score, you might be thinking that's a pretty high benchmark, but it's important to note that your score can vary quite a bit by age. Check out figure 2 to see where you stand among your peers.

Your actual age does not impact your credit or FICO score. But the age of your accounts and your payment history are taken into consideration. So if you're in your twenties, you are automatically at a disadvantage when it comes to your credit score, simply because of your lack of financial history. It's also assumed that individuals in their twenties will have larger amounts of debt, whether from student loans, new mortgages, or other financial obligations. That being said, it's no surprise consumers in their twenties have the lowest average credit score at 660. But it's assumed as you get older and more stable in your career, you will have an extensive, hopefully positive payment history and less debt. Between ages forty to sixty-nine, scores increase the most, jumping an average of twenty points in each decade. Keeping that in mind, individuals

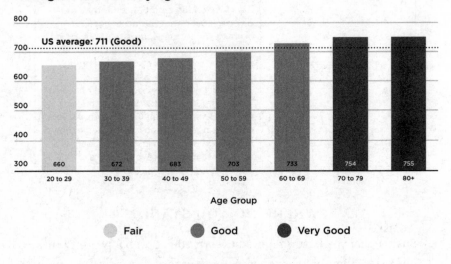

Average Credit Score by Age

US average: 711 (Good)

Age Group	Score
20 to 29	660
30 to 39	672
40 to 49	683
50 to 59	703
60 to 69	733
70 to 79	754
80+	755

Fair   Good   Very Good

Figure 2

seventy and older have the highest average credit scores, hovering around the 754 to 755 mark.

As a young person, it can be difficult to keep up with the high credit scores achieved by those who are retirement age. That's why as you develop your payment history over the course of your twenties, it should be part of your goal to also increase your credit score.

For some people, achieving the perfect credit score of 850 is a long-term goal, but it's more for the pleasure of knowing they have an 850 credit score. Attempting to achieve perfection may prohibit you from living your happiest, healthiest, and wealthiest life, so don't dwell on it! You would have to have the perfect ratio of credit usage and history to achieve this, which isn't easy. Truly, you can still achieve many of these same perks if your credit score is above 760, which is considered "very good" by banking institutions. According to MoneyGeek, approximately 58 percent of consumers with the perfect credit score of 850 are between the ages of fifty-six and seventy-four. This is largely due to increased income and decreased debt over time, compounded with a positive on-time payment history.

HAVE THAT CONVERSATION

If you're reading this book, maybe I know you or maybe I don't. Regardless of who you are, I just shared everything with you. I opened up my portfolio and showed you exactly where I stand in the world of credit. You can see my credit score, my credit usage, and how credit inquiries and not having any specific loans are negatively affecting my overall FICO score.

The reason I'm opening this up to you is because if you see my financial vulnerabilities, both good and bad, you will hopefully feel safer, in a place where you feel more comfortable telling me your financial vulnerabilities. Both good and bad. The less we can make this a taboo, the more we'll be better off. But it's not me you should be telling; it's your significant other, future significant other, or even loved ones. I hope you are slightly less afraid to start the conversation and Talk Money, or at least less afraid than you were at the start of this chapter.

So here's where you bear it all. Write down your credit score. Make it permanent. Maybe you're happy with your score, maybe you're a little disappointed. Either way, the important thing is now you know where you stand. You have the opportunity to put together a strategy for maintaining or improving your credit habits. Now share your score with your partner and encourage them to be a part of your strategy for the future. If you don't have a partner, this is a great way to practice for your future partner. Find a loved one, family member, or friend and throughout the book use these lines to practice with them.

_____   _____

My Credit Score   **My Partner's Score**

IT'S THE CLOSING BELL— HERE'S WHAT WE LEARNED

- Sharing your credit score with your partner, and having them do the same, is the most effective way to protect yourself from financial gaslighting.
- The difference in interest paid for a $300,000 home between the highest credit score range of 760 to 850 and the lower range of 620 to 639 over a thirty-year fixed-rate mortgage period is $110,626.31!
- You should pull your credit report annually, for free, on www.AnnualCreditReport.com. Make sure you review the report thoroughly and dispute any inaccuracies.

- You can pull your credit score from Experian. This is a soft inquiry and will not affect your credit! (www.experian.com/consumer-products/credit-score.html).
- The easiest way to boost your credit is to make payments on time. If you struggle with this, put your credit card and bills on autopay.
- The average FICO credit score for US citizens is 711.
- Share your credit report and score with your partner first. Being vulnerable with them will allow them to feel safe being vulnerable with you.

4

HOW MANY FINANCIAL ACCOUNTS DO YOU HAVE?

Avoiding Financial Deception

DING DING DING!!!
IT'S THE CHAPTER 4 OPENING BELL

- Your financial dating history. Say what?
- Financial deception in its purest form
- Who's talking about money in the fantasy suite?
- Understanding the importance of financial compatibility
- Building real financial transparency in your relationship
- Creating your personal financial statement
- Getting comfortable with the uncomfortable

When you start to date someone seriously, there are candid conversations about your dating history. Questions fly back and forth:

- How many long-term relationships have you been in?
- When did your last serious relationship end?

- Why did it end?
- What are you looking for in your next relationship?

These questions aren't meant to interrogate or judge your partner. Rather, the conversation is a way to gain understanding of your partner's emotional and relational history. Having these discussions is not only normal and common, but it strengthens your bond as a couple. The more we know about our significant other and the more we share with them, the deeper our understanding is of one another. And that's a beautiful thing.

In a similar way, you need to know your partner's financial dating history. So what the hell is that? Well, it's like someone's dating history, but instead of talking about exes, you're talking about finances. It leads to conversations of great depth filled with candor not only about our credit report and credit score but about where we keep our money and how much money we have borrowed.

Some questions to consider asking include:

- Which financial institutions do you use?
- Do you have retirement accounts set up yet?
- How much have you saved for retirement?
- How many total bank accounts do you have?
- Do you invest? How many total investment accounts do you have?
- In the last year, what were your lowest and highest balances?
- Do you use a safe or keep cash on hand?

You're probably thinking, *You really want me to ask these questions to my partner? This seems intrusive, Jason!* I'm not telling you to ask 'em on the first date. But if you're still uncertain, let me challenge you with this thought: the hesitation you're feeling is just a perception you have learned. Our society has ingrained what is and is not acceptable to ask others based on bullshit rules that only hold us back. I want to push you forward. We need to approach these conversations with our significant other the same way we approach conversations about our dating history—with compassion, patience, understanding, and without a shred of judgment.

Avoiding these conversations can have messy outcomes. By avoiding the money talk, we are unintentionally leaving the door open for gaps. These gaps often create an environment for financial deception. Financial deception can be anything as small as hiding the vanilla ice cream you snuck in on the way home to as large as hiding bank accounts, tax liens, cash, debt, or inherited investments.

Here is a lighthearted example from my own life on how I've seen people hide money from their spouse. I was at dinner with my parents and their family friends. It's two families, the kids are there, the dads are good buddies, the moms are friends, and I am sitting in the middle. My mother's friend leans over and whispers to my mom about a recent purchase she made, revealing that her hubby "doesn't know about *that* credit card." My mom, ever the ally, responds with, "Got it."

Actions similar to this happen so frequently that it has become an almost *normalized* part of relationships, even a funny joke to throw around over drinks. What I want to hammer home here is that we need to recognize this isn't behavior to normalize! Hiding bank accounts, purchases, cash, debt, and financial statements should not be accepted as tolerated behavior. We need to gain a sense of comfort with opening our portfolios and sharing the details with our significant other. No more hiding. No more games. No more secrets. Channel your inner Tom Cruise from *Jerry Maguire* and "Show me the *money*!" These conversations provoke authenticity, and as we know . . . authenticity is the driver of creating connection.

You might be thinking, *Isn't sharing our credit report with our partner enough, Jason?* It's an excellent and important step to understanding your significant other's baseline financial wellness.

But we need to dig deeper. On your credit report you see only the balances and payment history of how many outstanding, open, and closed credit institutions are associated with your identity. Specifically, the credit report doesn't track savings, checking, investment, retirement accounts, or even sidelined cash. Understanding your partner's **liquid assets** is just as important as understanding their delinquencies.

Every human walking has **assets** and **liabilities**. In the business world, a company will track this information through a **balance sheet**. It's a quick snapshot of the company's financial health and balances.[1] Every month or every quarter, the company's chief financial officer (CFO) will prepare an updated balance sheet to review and share with the business leaders in the company. This is a healthy financial practice. It's like going to the dentist twice a year to have your teeth cleaned. The dentist will poke around your mouth for a minute to make sure you don't have any cavities, give you a free toothbrush, and send you on your way. And while this isn't necessarily *fun*, it sure as hell beats blacklisting the dentist for years only to inevitably have twelve needle-injected doses of Novocain plunged into your gums and a whirring metal drill shoved in your cakehole. I mean, unless you're a sadist. The same thing can be said for the CFO who analyzes a company's balance sheet on a regular basis and shares this information with the other executives in the organization, investors outside the organization, and their lenders.

I want you to act like your own minibusiness—you are your CFO! Take control of understanding, balancing, analyzing, and managing your own assets and liabilities on a consistent basis. Why? Because it's a preventive measure. It's a way to ensure you're playing offense with your financial health, not defense. And buckle up, because in just a few pages you'll see what happens when you're playing defense.

Before moving forward, I want to be sure to include a very important caveat. The motive here is to get to full transparency so that you and your partner know each other's true financial picture, not to micromanage or control. This whole book, I've emphasized the importance of breaking down barriers, being vulnerable, and showcasing your portfolio with your partner, but I haven't really discussed when the conversation can go too far. None of us are perfect; it's difficult to judge when we've done enough, or if we've crossed a line, especially in the world of love and money. It's a balancing act between being open and honest and micromanaging every penny spent. That said, I want to make this loud and clear: you're stepping into financial vulnerability and, hopefully, so is your partner . . . don't weaponize this vulnerability!

Now let's firm up your understanding of assets and liabilities. An asset is anything you own or have **equity** in that can be of some economic value or liquidated for a value. This can include checking, savings, retirement, and investment accounts or physical property like real estate, a house, vehicle, jewelry, and so on. No matter what those old-school personal financial gurus say, that Gucci bag or belt is an asset.

A liability is considered a financial obligation, like a debt or loan instrument that you owe to a financial institution. To name a few, these can include credit cards, auto loans, mortgages, personal loans, or student loans. A general rule of thumb is to make sure your liabilities do not exceed your assets. But depending on your age and current financial status, your liabilities might exceed your assets, and that's okay. Sometimes we have to use debt as an investment in ourselves, such as a mortgage or student loan, to gain an asset like a home or career requiring an advanced degree. It's a balancing act without a one-size-fits-all solution.

Okay, now press pause.

Close your eyes and visualize your assets and liabilities.

Now open them, do some mental math, and ask yourself these honest questions:

Assets

- How many accounts do you have?
- Why do you have the accounts that you have?
- What does your retirement balance look like?
- What other assets do you own?
- What's the estimated value of those assets?

Liabilities

- How many liabilities do you have?
- What are their balances?
- How long until they are repaid?
- Are most of your liabilities tied to your assets?

How healthy does your personal balance sheet look? Is it skewed toward assets or liabilities? It matters, but at this point, right now, this second, we can push it to the side. I want to get your wheels turning, to have you start thinking about what you own and what you owe. The biggest piece to healthy financial behavior is simply having a high-level understanding of your current portfolio before making any day-to-day financial decisions.

Once you have your arms wrapped around what your assets and liabilities are, I want you to become very comfortable with this information. For my therapy-goers, this is like finally finding your inner child and pulling that tiny, elusive shit out of the dustiest corner of your psyche and into the light. It's the moment when the dual roles of hider and seeker morph into the latter and everything clicks. Step one is to do the work to better understand yourself, step two is to grow as a human, and step three is to become comfortable enough to share it with those you trust. Get mentally prepared to share this information with your partner, just like the CFO shares the balance sheet with the other executives in the company and outside investors. In order to grow from a personal and financial perspective, we need to get comfortable with discussing the uncomfortable. If a CFO fails to share the company's financial status with shareholders and that balance sheet is upside down, he will be fired, and the organization may go out of business. When you fail to be financially transparent with your partner, and vice versa, those actions can have dire consequences. To showcase the importance of money morality, we're going to delve into a story of real-life financial deception in action. This one is nuts!

REAL-LIFE FINANCIAL DECEPTION IN ACTION

I had the pleasure of interviewing a listener of *Trading Secrets* who, unfortunately, was the victim of financial deception in a romantic relationship. For legal reasons, she has chosen to remain anonymous. For the sake of unoriginality, let's refer to her as Jane Doe. Her story is a wild one, so buckle up.

Jason: Thank you so much for your time. I hear you have a crazy financial deception story for us.

Jane: Yes, this is actually a ten-year saga that started around 2011. I was twenty-four, dating my ex, who was ten years older than me. I was head over heels. We decided to buy a house together after a year of dating. While we were under contract to buy the house, he convinced me to add him to all of my bank accounts. He said it would look "better" to the banks if all the money was coming out of one account. So, being young, dumb, and in love, I added him to my accounts. Technically, our down payment came from our "joint" account, but all the money accumulated was mine. He never contributed any of his own money for the deposit.

Jason: So if all the money for the down payment was yours, why didn't you just purchase the home instead of adding his name to the deed?

Jane: At the time, I was making $50,000 as a financial adviser and was just starting my career. He was making $85,000 as a property manager. The reason I didn't just buy the house on my own is because, even though I had the money for the down payment, I needed his income to apply for the loan because he was making more.

Jason: That makes complete sense. Then what happened?

Jane: As we were going through the process of getting a loan for the home, I found out that my ex hadn't filed his taxes since 2003. So I footed a $1,200 bill to pay off his back taxes. I had a nagging feeling in my gut that signing for the house was a bad idea. But I pushed that feeling aside because I really thought he was the one.

Jason: Did the bank approve the mortgage and was the closing finalized?

Jane: Yes. We ended up closing in November 2012. Everything was okay, initially. Less than two months after moving in, I went to get the mail and saw a letter from the IRS addressed to my ex. Inside was a $57,000 **tax lien** on our brand-new house! I footed a $1,200 bill to pay his back taxes off; I knew nothing about the $57,000 tax lien. The tax lien ended up being from my ex's previous marriage in 2003. He hadn't owned anything strategically until this point because he knew in his criminal mind that a tax lien would be placed on that asset. Clearly, I didn't know this existed.

Jason: Oh my god! What did he say when you confronted him?

Jane: He pretty much said something to the effect of, "Oh yeah, I didn't think that the tax lien would matter because you and I are going to be together forever, and this is going to be our forever home." I was so mad. It does matter! He should have been transparent and told me before we bought the home. Now his financial missteps are affecting me.

Jason: You're absolutely right, he should have been up front with you. After you found it, did you immediately end it?

Jane:, It was the straw that broke the camel's back. We broke up shortly after, and I kicked him out of the house. My ex was not only deceptive in the financial sense but in every way.

Jason: How did you pull yourself out of the situation after the breakup?

Jane: I wanted to sell the house, but my ex refused because he wanted the tax lien to fall off in 2016. He said we could look into selling it then. I decided to make the house a rental property to help pay for the mortgage. My ex never contributed a dollar to the upkeep or the mortgage. In September 2013, I started dating my now husband, and he was an incredible help with the house. He helped me manage the rental property and dig into the details behind the tax lien. From 2013 to 2017, my husband and I moved to Florida and had a long-term renter for the house. During that time, I didn't have much contact with my ex. Eventually, the renters moved out, and my husband and I moved back to Denver and lived briefly in the rental home while we searched for our own house. In 2017, my husband and I approached my ex about selling the house again. He refused. The original $57,000 tax lien had fallen off, but three more tax liens were added. Their individual amounts were approximately $33,000, $17,000, and $15,000.

Jason: That is awful! When were the liens set to fall off?

Jane: Not until 2024. My husband and I decided not to continue down this path. We found out we were pregnant with twins and needed to get out of this situation. In March 2021, ten years after I first started dating my ex, we hired an attorney. After six months of back-and-forth and $30,000 in attorney fees, my lawyer got my ex to settle for $60,000. I think that was the worst part of this whole experience: writing him a huge check when he didn't put a penny into the property and causing years of havoc in my life. So, in total, we ended up paying $90,000 in fees and settlement.

Jason: I am so sorry you had to deal with that. Catch me up—why did you have to write your ex a check?

Jane: Both our names were on the deed, so it was a joint asset. As a result, he was entitled to 50 percent of the assets. But our attorney ended up getting him to settle for less, which is why we wrote the $60,000 check.

Jason: What ever happened to the tax liens?

Jane: A few weeks before we settled, he also settled his tax lien with the IRS through an offer in compromise, which allows you to settle your debt for less than the full amount you owe. So instead of the $60,000 we paid him going toward the tax lien, my ex ended up pocketing that money.

Jason: Wow. Knowing what you know now, what would you have done differently to prevent this scenario?

Jane: There are obviously so many things I would have done differently. First and foremost, I would have run a credit report on my ex to see what loans and liabilities he had outstanding. Second, I would have listened to my gut. There were so many red flags I just blatantly ignored because I was in love. Even though this story is crazy, it has a happy ending. My husband and I are happy and have a great family, we ended up selling the rental house at a profit, and we are no longer tied to my terrible ex.

Jason: I'm so happy to hear that your story ended positively. Hopefully sharing your story will prevent even just one person from falling victim to the same trap! Thank you for sharing with us!

A nightmare story that is more common than you think. I will tell you this, my email inbox was absolutely flooded when I asked my audience if they had experienced financial deception from their partners. Hopefully after hearing Jane's story, you understand the importance of financial transparency and laying all your cards on the table before taking the next step, like buying a house, with your partner. And if you don't have a significant other right now, you're at the very least prepared for what's to come! When you boil it down, choosing your lifelong partner is one of the most important financial decisions you'll ever have to make. When you move in together, not only are you bringing boxes of clothes and dishes, you're also bringing your financial baggage too. That's why having money chemistry is equally as important as financial transparency.

ARE YOU HERE FOR THE RIGHT REASONS?

It's the iconic question commonly asked on *The Bachelor* and on most dating shows. In an age where ghosting and deception are prevalent, we are constantly seeking validation when we're dating. We guard our hearts and only reveal our deepest fears, thoughts, and ambitions when we feel we can really trust the other person— preferably as far away from a camera lens as possible. There's a series of things we do to gain this trust and validation. Going on dates, meeting each other's friends and family, and learning how to navigate difficult conversations.

We do everything in our power to make sure the other person is here for the right reasons *before* making the relationship official. Do we have chemistry? Are we emotionally compatible? Do we share the same morals and values? On *The Bachelor*, there's such an emphasis on emotional compatibility, which is important, but there's no emphasis on financial compatibility. I mean, really, who is talking about their finances in the fantasy suite?

Trista Sutter is the OG Bachelorette. Literally the first Bachelorette in the show's history, and holy shit was it successful! We're talking more than fifty million viewers when that baby aired in 2003. It was the biggest season the franchise has ever had ratings wise. Numbers that were inches—scratch that—*centimeters* away from what the series finale of *Friends* drew. Ryan and Trista are a marquee couple that everyone in Bachelor Nation tries to emulate. Their commitment and love for each other is really something special.

I am lucky enough to call Trista and Ryan friends. In 2022, I went on an amazing trip to Curaçao with them. Over dinner and drinks, I was talking to Trista and asked her, "I'm writing a second book based on the relationship between love and money, and I was hoping you could help me. In the fantasy suites did you talk about money, finances, career, credit, or anything in that realm?" She laughed and said, "Absolutely not!" Then she made the comment "It's all about chemistry! That's all I was looking for in the fantasy suites. Once there's that, then the next steps are potentially talking about career, finances, and money, but I'm not getting to that point until we find out if we are compatible."

I totally agree with Trista here. You need to find out if you can dance before you pick your dance partner. If your partner wants to tango and you want to foxtrot, it may not work out! Chemistry and intimacy are such a huge part of the relationship equation. There's no argument there. But I want to challenge you with this thought: being on the same page with your partner, professionally and financially, has been proven to be a common sticking point in relationships.

Remember that poll from the National Endowment for Financial Education where 43 percent of individuals with combined finances committed some form of financial deception?[2] This can range from hiding a purchase, cash, bank accounts, credit cards, or lying about debt or earnings. According to a recent study conducted by Ramsey Solutions, financial incompatibility and money fights are the second leading cause of divorce, right next to marital infidelity.[3] As a society, we are conditioned to be hyperaware of our partner's potential infidelity, but we are actively turning a blind eye to the number two reason people are getting divorced! Why are we not talking about this more? Why are we not taking a more proactive approach to love and money? Knowing that a large percentage of couples struggle with navigating the financial waters, why would you choose to ignore it?

While you may have the chemistry piece down, you can't overlook your financial compatibility. If you do, you're potentially jeopardizing your intimacy and emotional connection. Just like when you ask someone their dating history, what struggles they've been through, and what long-term relationship didn't work out and why, we need to get comfortable with probing for financial compatibility. Where do you keep your money? What types of accounts do you have? What are the balances in those accounts? What is the succession plan? Because hiding from that is as alarming as not being able to dance in the fantasy suite.

After my conversation with Trista, curiosity got the best of me. I wanted to know if any leads in Bachelor Nation world discussed finances or careers during their time in the fantasy suite. Here's what I found:

- Trista Sutter: Had three fantasy suites and discussed money with zero of her dates.
- Kaitlyn Bristowe: Had four fantasy suites and discussed money with zero of her dates.
- Clayton Echard: Had two fantasy suites and discussed money with zero of his dates.
- Ben Higgins: Had four fantasy suites and discussed money with zero of his dates. In Ben's words, "Never once did money come up; the only thing that came close to it was opportunities outside of the show. I did have one girl ask me how much I was paid to be The Bachelor."
- Bob Guiney: Had four fantasy suites and discussed money with zero of his dates. In Bob's words, "Out of all of my fantasy suites, zero involved any conversation around

credit, debt, and future finances at all. Now looking back on it, fantasy suites were too surface level and not good prep work for a life partner."

- Peter Weber: Had three fantasy suites and discussed money with one of his dates.

Peter is the only one of our surveyed group that discussed anything in the realm of money or career. That's only one date out of a total of twenty fantasy suites. This is a small sample size of just a few leads, but it was interesting that just days before potentially being engaged, money and financial topics in these instances were never addressed. I share this because they are not alone. I truly believe this is a realistic snapshot of the macroeconomics when it comes to money conversations before saying "I do."

FINANCIAL COMPATIBILITY

You probably have heard the saying "You gotta test the car before you buy it." This is an old adage when referring to picking your partner. While it's important to test-drive a car, for all the obvious reasons, I want to take this analogy a step further.

Before moving on to the next step, you need to know how the car is financed. Are you paying cash? Leasing? Financing? What is the interest rate? That might sound weird, but if you find you aren't compatible with the car financially, then it doesn't really matter if you like the way the car looks, handles, or how much horsepower is under the engine. If you forgot to laugh there, then your finance hat is definitely on tight, and I am here for that! This same thought process can be applied when choosing your life partner.

So, how do you know if you and your partner are financially compatible? In my eyes, if I am open and honest with you about my financial status, and in return, you are open and honest with me, the hard part is over. The veil is lifted and there is no more front, no more bullshit, no more mystery. We may not have the same exact views on spending, saving, earning, working, and investing, but if we're able to be vulnerable with each other about our money status, without judgment or fighting, chances are, we are at least each other's dance partner.

When it comes to love and money, you and your partner *do not* have to carry identical views. Rather, you need to be able to communicate about your financial fears and goals to ensure you both are on the same page. In any relationship there's always a give and a take. One partner might be messy, the other might be a neat freak. The messy partner tries to be conscientious of leaving their clothes on the floor and the neat freak tries to let go of their need to clean the bathroom twice a day. In the same way, one partner might love to cook, so in return the other partner does the dishes. These are normal compromises we already make in our relationships. We need to treat our finances in the same way. One person might be a heavy spender and the other person might be frugal. As a compromise, the spender agrees to discuss any purchases over an agreed-upon dollar amount with their partner before issuing the transaction, and the frugal partner agrees to stop monitoring every latte purchased at Starbucks. Not only will these compromises give you and your significant other peace of mind, but you will trust each other more, because there are no secrets.

FINANCIAL DECEPTION = INFIDELITY

So what happens if you are open and honest with your partner about your financial status, but they aren't open with you? Well, my friend, that is a huge red flag. Maybe something deeper is going on with your partner. Maybe they are self-conscious of their debt, spending, or balances. Maybe they were raised in a home where money wasn't discussed. There can be a million and one reasons for their hesitation, and quite honestly, I'm not able or qualified to diagnose the specific cause. But I urge you to marinate on this thought: deception is mitigated by transparency.

Let's get comfortable showcasing our financial portfolio. Just like we showcase our résumé to a potential employer. Just like *Bachelor* contestants make sure there's chemistry in the fantasy suites. Just like we want to make sure there is emotional compatibility when we're dating. It's my belief that intentionally cheating with finances is the equivalent of having an affair. You may disagree with that thinking, but let's table it.

How can you avoid financial infidelity and deception? You can avoid it by opening your portfolio. I'm not telling you to go on a Hinge date and three days later share your bank statement. You're already dating or sharing a life or sharing a house with somebody you love, or thinking about taking that next step. I'm just asking you to push a little further, to open the vault and to let your partner take a peek inside.

If you and your partner are on the same page financially and you know where the accounts are, there is no need to hide cash or purchases. If you find out your spouse is hiding money, the automatic reaction is, "What else are you hiding?" I'm not a relationship expert, but this isn't a huge leap. Money issues can fracture the relationship's foundation, threatening your love and trust for each other.

According to the National Endowment for Financial Education, in those 43 percent of couples where there was financial deception, 18 percent ended up breaking up or divorcing over it.[4] Holy shit!

It's pretty easy to define cheating on a significant other. We've all seen romantic comedies about the guy or girl who makes an indiscretion at a party, the love of their life finds out, and then the cheater spends the rest of the movie trying to win back the one that got away. But what exactly is financial cheating? According to Investopedia, financial cheating or infidelity occurs when couples with combined finances lie to each other about money.[5] Specifically, one partner might have significant debt on a credit card their partner is unaware of, or similarly, a partner might have a secret, separate checking account. Making large, discretionary purchases, like buying a new set of Titleist golf clubs without discussing it with your partner, is considered a form of financial infidelity. Or, even worse, they have $57,000 in debt to the IRS!

In the age of technology, spotting signs of financial cheating has become increasingly difficult. Nowadays, most people receive their bank statements electronically rather than receive hard copies in the mail. If your partner has a separate email account, it's very easy for them to keep potential invoices and statements a secret. For individuals who struggle with managing money, this behavior can result in tens of thousands of dollars amassed in debt. Another red flag could be large, unexplained withdrawals from a joint account, or checks that are made out to cash.[6] When you don't know, you assume, and when large consistent cash withdrawals are made without explanation, one may assume a drugs or gambling problem. Finally, another common sign of financial cheating is defensiveness around the subject of money. If your partner shuts down or pulls away from discussions around finances, this is usually a good indicator that something is awry.

If you or your partner has committed financial infidelity, the best thing to do is to come clean. To air out all the dirty laundry and accept responsibility for your actions. If you are the victim of financial cheating, the easy reaction is to blow up. But that's not always the *right* reaction. As a partner, sometimes the best thing you can do is listen and create a plan for the future. There's no use in dwelling on the money spent and the purchases made. That money is gone out the window. The best thing, and really the only thing, that can be done is to make sure this behavior doesn't occur again.

1. Put all of your accounts on the table and open up your portfolio. Share access and don't hide the balances or debt.
2. Consider hiring a bookkeeper, CPA, or financial planner, adviser, or manager to manage your taxes, investments, and retirement accounts. You can even use apps or robo-advisors. For the tech-savvy, those details are to come in chapter 10.

3. See a financial therapist *together*. A financial therapist combines practical money-handling advice with psychological strategies to help individuals and couples gain clarity on the emotional side of money management and how it may be negatively affecting their lives. The only way to fix an issue is to consistently work toward improvement.

FINANCIAL TRANSPARENCY

Just like I've done throughout the entirety of this book, I'm going to get vulnerable and be completely transparent with you. I'll show you my cards so that you can feel comfortable showing your cards to your partner. It's a great cycle we have going on here, right? Well, I want you to track three items and share this information with your partner:

1. how many accounts
2. types of accounts
3. balances in each account

Accounts will likely land in one of these three buckets: banking, borrowing, or investing. In summary, these accounts will hold balances that are assets or liabilities. For now, start by checking the account you currently have:

- **Banking and Cash**
  - Checking Account _____
  - Savings Account _____
  - Money Market Account _____
  - Certificate of Deposit (CD) _____
  - Cash Account _____

- **Borrowing and Credit**
  - Personal Loan _____
  - Car Loan _____
  - Mortgage Loan _____
  - Student Loan _____
  - Credit Card Account _____
  - Line of Credit _____

- **Individual Retirement Account**
  - Traditional _____
  - Roth _____
  - SEP _____
  - SIMPLE _____

- **Employer Retirement Account**
  - 401(k) _____
  - 403(b) _____

- **Other Tax-Advantaged Accounts**
  - Health Savings Account (HSA) _____
  - Education Savings Account (ESA) _____

- **Other Miscellaneous Accounts**
  - Brokerage Account _____
  - Trust Account _____
  - Joint Account _____
  - Insurance (beyond the fire, water, home, auto, and other mandatory forms) _____

- **Business Accounts**
  - ○ Checking Account _____
  - ○ Savings Account _____
  - ○ Credit Card Account _____

To give you an idea, between business accounts, personal accounts, investment accounts, retirement accounts, and credit cards, I have a total of thirty-four different accounts. Yes, thirty-four! I would not recommend this as it takes an army to keep the organization tight. That said, for every account I have, I can justify the value it brings to me and/or my business. You should be able to do the same. And remember, you're officially your own CFO, so if you have accounts that are not serving value to your financial organization, consolidate.

Maybe if you're a business owner or entrepreneur, you also have upward of twenty or thirty different types of accounts . . . maybe even more. But even if you don't run a business, at some point it may make sense to have multiple bank accounts.

The Federal Deposit Insurance Company, or **FDIC**, is a government agency that regulates financial institutions and helps consumers feel confident in placing their money in FDIC-insured banks. As of 2023, FDIC insurance guarantees protection of your funds only through $250,000. If you have exposure greater than $250,000 in a bank, you can diversify your funds. Check the current FDIC insurance because they may increase the amount in the future. In 2008 there was a temporary increase from the $100,000 limit to $250,000, which then became a permanent limit in July of 2010. So it's been ten-plus years since an increase; expect one soon![7] Spread out your wealth through multiple banks so that none of your cash is left uninsured. Figure 3 is a breakdown of the coverage limits directly from the FDIC.

FDIC Deposit Insurance Coverage Limits by Account Ownership Category	
Single Accounts (Owned by One Person)	$250,000 per owner
Joint Accounts (Owned by Two or More Persons)	$250,000 per co-owner
Certain Retirement Accounts (Includes IRAs)	$250,000 per owner
Revocable Trust Accounts	$250,000 per owner per unique beneficiary
Corporation, Partnership, and Unincorporated Association Accounts	$250,000 per corporation, partnership, or unincorporated association
Irrevocable Trust Accounts	$250,000 for the noncontingent interest of each unique beneficiary
Employee Benefit Plan Accounts	$250,000 for the noncontingent interest of each plan participant
Government Accounts	$250,000 per official custodian (more coverage available subject to specific conditions)

Figure 3

While it might be more difficult to manage, it's good to have multiple bank accounts, especially if you are close to or over that $250,000 insurance limit. And if you like shopping, shop the banks. Pin them against one another to see who will give you the best rates. Most important, know where the accounts are. If you are having trouble keeping track of your accounts, we need to create a system to organize that information. Considering I have thirty-four different accounts, I understand the struggle. But with that struggle, I have an automated system for analysis, balancing, investing, budgeting, and tax planning! The number of accounts doesn't have anything to do with your financial well-being; it has to do with understanding the entirety of your financial picture. You can't manage and lead your financial freedom without understanding where every square inch of it lies.

UNDERSTAND YOUR PFS

I'm going to share a pro tip with you that I learned from my time as a corporate banker. There's a document called a personal financial statement (PFS) that breaks down an individual's total assets and liabilities. The PFS can help track an individual's financial goals as well as detail their total net worth.[8] When as a banker we would lend money to companies, we would require the owner to provide their PFS because we might take a **personal guarantee** on their assets. In nonbanker jargon, if the company defaulted on their loan, we would hold the owner's assets as collateral. And those assets are listed on their personal financial statement.

Every time I analyzed an owner's PFS for a loan, I was always surprised. There's never a way to back into it. There's no hiding. Why? Because numbers don't lie. The business owner with the luxury foreign car, country club membership, and $2,000 suit sometimes would have the most amount of bad debt on their balance sheet. Sometimes the most unassuming business owner with the most basic business had the most assets. Now this was when I worked in the business segment, but even when I worked in the retail segment, the same held true. You've heard the phrase before, but it bears repeating: don't judge a book by its cover. Covers can lie, numbers don't, and these numbers can tell us the whole story. A perfect example of this is detailed by a 2022 study conducted by Experian Automotive. In their research they found most wealthy people aren't driving around in a Rolls-Royce. In fact, it's exactly the opposite. According to the study, 61 percent of individuals with a household income greater than $250,000 drive Toyotas, Fords, and Hondas, just like the average Joe.[9]

Reflecting on all of this made me think, *Why don't we all understand our PFS and our partner's PFS?* Be honest with me—have you completed your PFS in the last few months? Or, for that matter, ever? Purely from an organizational standpoint, it helps you keep up with which accounts you have, the institutions you use, and the respective balances of those accounts. This is exactly the method I use to keep track of my assets and my liabilities. On the last day of every month, I log into each of my thirty-four accounts and track their balances in an Excel workbook. It takes less than ten minutes to update and helps me stay on top of my professional and personal financial goals. I created a similar format for you in the sample PFS.

Sample PFS

Assets	Amount
Cash—Checking	
Cash—Savings	
Emergency Fund	
Retirement Fund	
Investment Fund	
Personal Property	
Real Estate	
Automobile	
Other (Jewelry, Watches, Furniture)	
Total Assets:	
Liabilities	**Amount**
Credit Card #1	
Credit Card #2	
Student Loan	
Mortgage/Rent	
Automobile Loan	
Health-Care loan	
Unpaid Taxes	
Personal Loan	
Other	
Total Liabilities:	

My Total Accounts	_____
My Total Assests	_____
My Total Liabilities	_____
My Net Worth (Total Assets − Total Liabilities)	_____

I challenge you to write this information down and get it out in the open. It takes the guesswork out of the equation. You know exactly where you stand as far as how many accounts you possess and their balances down to the penny. We're setting ourselves up for success. So, just like when I was a banker and I saw business owners' personal financial statements and their accounts, you need to see yours for yourself, and you need to understand these details for your partner.

While insurance is not necessarily an account you monitor and track the balances of, it's important to understand what types of insurance you carry and the succession plans behind those coverages. It's doubly important that your significant other understands what coverages you carry in case of an emergency and vice versa. Common insurance coverages to consider carrying are life, personal umbrella, health, renters or homeowners, and auto. When it comes to life insurance, the holder will need to name a beneficiary. Maybe now is a good time to consider if you and your partner should name each other as beneficiaries on the insurance. Or if you would rather list a dependent or parent as a beneficiary, it might be time to reveal that information to your partner. In the same vein, if you and your partner are cohabitating, you might consider creating one joint insurance package. You'd be surprised by how much you can save if you and your significant other wrap each other's liabilities under one policy. You may even qualify for a multiline discount if you carry two or more policies with the same insurance company. Whether you track your insurance coverages on the PFS or just have an open conversation about the coverages, it's important for you and your partner to know where the accounts are and the succession plans behind them.

DO NOT WEAPONIZE FINANCIAL VULNERABILITY

Hopefully by now you've rolled up your sleeves, done the work, and had the conversation with your partner. Was it as tough and scary as you thought? Even if it was tough and scary, do you feel a sense of relief knowing that you and your partner are now on the same page financially? My sincere hope is that you and your partner now have peace of mind. Relationships aren't easy, but if we put in the effort, our connection as a couple will be exponentially stronger.

Early in this chapter I warned against using this vulnerability as a way to micromanage or control. Here's a practical way to prevent micromanaging finances with your partner. When you start the conversation about sharing your account information with each other, set a precedent on how often you want to do a checkup. Maybe it's like the dentist, twice a year. It's important for you to check your own accounts monthly, via the PFS we discussed. Customize your system, making sure it fits a time frame that works for both of your needs and wants. It's important to keep these checkup conversations straightforward and brief. The bottom line is to make sure the accounts are trending upward. Without showcasing our numbers to our partner and having them reciprocate, it's impossible to gauge each other's financial wellness. We want our partner to be healthy physically and mentally so they can lead a happy, long life. We should put the same emphasis on each other's financial wellness. If our finances are in disarray, it can affect our emotional and physical lives, sticking its ugly head up in the form of arguments and stress. Take control of your financial wellness and share your numbers with each other. Numbers don't lie. The sooner we wrap our arms around our numbers, and our partner's numbers, the sooner we can kiss financial deception goodbye.

Pull out your personal financial statement and open your portfolio. Show them where your money is and how much you have. Now ask them if they would be willing to reciprocate. I've already shown you the doom and gloom reality of couples who avoid money talks. Don't be another statistic. Take the plunge and have a conversation with your partner.

My Total Accounts	My Partner's Total Accounts

IT'S THE CLOSING BELL— IN THIS CHAPTER WE COVERED

- Avoiding the money talk is a breeding ground for potential financial deception.
- Financial deception can include something as small as hiding a purchase, or as big as hiding a bank account or massive credit card debt. Don't let deception be the middleman in your relationship.
- Financial capability is equally as important as emotional capability, no matter what reality TV tells you.
- FDIC insurance, which is provided by most reputable banking institutions, only guarantees protection of your funds up to $250,000. If you're close to this number, open another bank account for maximum security.
- Assets are things you own or have equity in, like a house or car. Liabilities are things you owe, like a student loan or credit card debt. It's critical to understand your own assets and liabilities before starting the money talk with your partner. You can keep track of these through the personal financial statement.
- Don't use your partner's vulnerability as a way to micromanage their money decisions.

5

WHAT ARE YOUR ANNUAL EXPENSES?

Money Can't Buy You Love, But It Can Buy You a Mess!

DING DING DING!!!
IT'S THE CHAPTER 5 OPENING BELL

- What are your spending triggers?
- How to play financial defense
- The psychology behind spending
- Saving or spending? Nothing wrong with either!
- Let's talk about the 2 Dozen Jack Rule
- How to keep your variable and fixed expenses in check

We have a problem in this country, and it starts and ends with s-p-e-n-d-i-n-g. But of course we do. The majority of our country's GDP is made from consumer spending. So who the hell is incentivized to tell us to stop? *No one.* Just like the casino isn't going to stop us from playing the slot machine—that is, until we run out of cash. We need to stop worrying about being rich, obsessing over wanting more, and comparing ourselves to the posts and reels we see on Instagram and TikTok. We will never acquire that type of wealth until we make a true commitment to understanding our financial patterns, behaviors, and triggers.

This understanding will be the starting point to mastering our financial defense and instrumental in building wealth. When it comes to spending, *you* need to understand *you*. Because your spending triggers are different from your partner's, and the only way to improve financial health as a couple is to first work on yourself. If you and your partner are saving for a big purchase and you can't control your Amazon addiction, you'll likely cause a rift in your relationship. This will help us break the curse of spending more than we make, so let's get ahead of it and figure out your spending triggers.

- How often do you impulsively shop?
- Do you overspend during the holidays?
- Do iPhone banner ad sales or email blasts sucker you into spending?
- Do you over-purchase to stockpile?
- Do you use coupons or discount codes just because they came across your way?
- Does alcohol consumption lead you to make impulse purchases?
- Do you overspend at restaurants or bars?

This practice is about spending self-awareness. If you found yourself answering yes to any of these questions, you're off to a good start in spotting some red flags to your spending patterns. Most humans subconsciously overspend. They are spending without recognizing that they are falling into traps of overspending.

Three Reason Why People Subconsciously Overspend

1. The satisfaction and excitement over acquiring something new
2. FOMOD: fear of missing out on the deal
3. An endorphin attachment to the process or product

Hopefully, you're starting to identify your patterns and behaviors that align with subconscious overspending. Now that you're doing the full drill-down, I need you to do a little behavioral-based budgeting. This is *not* a tortuous exercise in which you sit down at the end of the week with a pen, paper, or spreadsheet marking down every coffee you bought. Behavioral-based budgeting is like asking questions on a date in the hope that you don't catch any red flags. Only instead of asking your date, you're asking yourself. Yes, I'm asking you to date yourself, at least from a financial perspective. Start by analyzing your bank statements, paying close attention to where you're spending. Look for the red flags here. What sticks out? What doesn't make much sense? Which purchase makes you stop and say, "What the hell is that!" Identify those red flags. Then ask yourself why.

- What is the meaning behind your spending?
- Does social pressure influence your spending habits?
- Are you trying to put on a persona you think might impress people?
- Does emotion control your credit card swipes?
- Are you having FOMOD?
- Is there a possible internal ego battle?

We need to understand what is going on and why. In the spirit of full transparency, I did this exercise in my early twenties, and I found I was spending an ungodly amount of money at bars. I mean, in 2010, I was making $45,000 my first year out of college and my dumb ass was spending more than $2,000 a month on alcohol! After a couple of years of overspending like an ass clown, I finally had the wherewithal to look within and asked myself, "Why?" Well, I was feeling insecure out of college. I wasn't sure of my direction. I wasn't certain I was "making it" by the standard of society. I wasn't sure I was in the right job. I questioned my location. And as my insecurities grew, so did my spending at bars.

Throwing my card down and saying, "Drinks on me, boys!" allowed me to feel confident and secure because of the reaction from my friends and acquaintances. The perception that I was doing well enough to afford the $300, $400, $500 bill at the end of the night was more intoxicating than the booze. Once I understood that, I started taking care of myself and identifying my impulsive spending behaviors. I recognized I didn't need to overspend at bars to make myself feel full or gain the respect of my friends. I could find fulfillment in other ways. Once I started working on myself and my deeper issues, my financial decisions improved. No more open bar tabs for the boys. And without even knowing it, there I was . . . playing a solid game of financial defense, putting myself in a better financial position.

There are really two perspectives to our money behavior; it's almost like we're playing a game here. Football, hockey, soccer, tennis, any type of sporting event you watch, has offense and defense. Financial offense is the act of generating cash inflows, which we call income. Financial defense is how we manage the cash outflows, or what we spend our dollars on. Imagine this—there's two minutes left on the clock, our team is up by a touchdown, but the opponent is in the red zone. How do we stop them from scoring? Well-disciplined, well-coached, and well-executed defense, of course. Our team has studied the opponent's offense, and we understand their playbook. Now we have to put that knowledge to the test. We must anticipate the opponent's next move before they make it, giving our team time to react, defend, and keep the lead. That's defense in the sports world, and that's our strategy for financial defense as it relates to spending. Every great coach, player, or hall-of-fame athlete stands by the popular line "defense wins championships." Financial defense is managing your spending by understanding and anticipating your spending triggers, and the championship is your wealth accumulation.

THE PSYCHOLOGY OF SPENDING

There's a stigma out there that all spending is bad. I am here to break that. Spending can be incredible and rewarding. But I have one simple rule: don't spend like an asshole! I'll define that later, but for now take this in . . . the average American household spends 82 percent of their after-tax income. The average US household income is approximately $84,000. That's the equivalent of spending more than $61,000 a year.[1]

Approximately $3,780 of that is spent on utilities. I'm talking about basic stuff, like electricity, water, gas, and sewer. The price of goods and services are at a forty-year high and climbing, leaving you with less money in your bank account.[2] These statistics are not a scare tactic; they're just spending facts that are real. It's normal to spend and—news flash—we spend too damn much!

We're all in the same boat here. There are expenses that we *can't* control, like the rising cost of food, electricity, utilities, housing, and gas. But at the same time, there are expenses we *can* control, like traveling, dining, and shopping. We can't control the nature of the current economic cycle we're living in, but we can focus on the controllables. Specifically, the psychology and behaviors behind what we spend our money on and why.

Our spending habits change and evolve as we grow personally and professionally. Think about what you were spending money on three, five, ten, or fifteen years ago. Maybe three to five years ago you didn't live with your significant other. Maybe ten years ago you didn't have a family. Maybe fifteen years ago you were still in school and were waiting tables. As we age, our income changes, our responsibilities change, and even our values change. Our spending habits are a direct reflection of those changes. We can analyze so much about the entirety of our lives just by what we purchase.

As you know by now, I like to keep it basic when it comes to personal finance. So to dissect spending we have to actually understand it. Simply put, spending, whether paying your rent or buying a concert ticket, is the action of exchanging money for a good or service that you want or need. My wants and needs are different from yours. That doesn't mean I'm right and you're wrong; it just means we're different. And it's likely your spending will be different from your loved ones, which is normal!

If you hold the mentality that spending is bad, I want you to change your perception on money handling. Think about it this way: If you're an employee and you work extremely hard for your company and show positive results, do you think you deserve a raise? The answer is probably yes. In order to qualify for that raise, your company has to *spend* more of their money on you. The company will likely view this expenditure as a long-term investment. By *spending more*, they assume you will continue to provide great results for years to come, because you are an *asset* to the company.

When spending is used strategically, you can end up receiving more in return than you spent. This applies not only monetarily but emotionally as well. Dinner out with your friends can provide a positive emotional return, even if it looks like a deficit in your bank account. Just like dressing sharp for an interview may have an impact on the offer they send. You get it. The spending box is officially checked.

Let's get into the subconscious overspending. Subconscious overspending is when your outflows unintentionally exceed your inflows. It's a pattern that often goes unidentified, but it's one that must immediately be corrected. That said, overspending will happen at times and can be justified, like when buying a car, a house, or paying for an emergency medical bill. The necessity is recognizing *when* and *why* it's occurring.

Typically, when you do something wrong, you know it. I remember the first time I was yelled at in kindergarten for stealing my friend Lynn's pickle at lunchtime. I can still feel those butterflies in my stomach when I was yelled at. It was my first sprinkle of anxiety, and I was shaken up. When you do something involving deception, manipulation, or something just flat out wrong, do you recognize it? Can you feel it in your gut? When it comes to overspending, for the most part, we realize when we cross the proverbial line. When we go outside of our spending limits. When we make an impulse purchase purely based on emotion. Deep down we know it; we just usually choose to ignore it.

When it comes to taking control of our finances, especially in volatile times, I want to reduce the emotional, trigger purchases. I'm not saying those purchases are necessarily negative, but I want to encourage you to take a beat and think before you press purchase or swipe the card.

Being intentional with your spending is a work of art that evolves into money mindfulness. It's a mechanism that you must understand and utilize—to be mindful of your money and the purchases you're making. It really boils down to one question: Are you aware of what you're spending as it relates to what you earn?

Before we take out spreadsheets and pencils and link every credit card to every finance guru's app, we should first focus on understanding our money habits. We can analyze data all day long, but what really drives that information is our learned habits and behaviors. I want you to get into the weeds and understand the psychology and decision-making process behind your spending habits.

Knowing the habits you've developed and where and why they show up is the key to changing those habits. Only you can answer these questions. Are you aware when you're overspending? If you're not, I will provide you the tools to help you get there, but first let's identify if you're a saver or a spender.

SPENDER OR SAVER?
NOTHING WRONG WITH EITHER

There's this idea that if you're a saver, you have your life figured out. You're the king or the queen sitting on a throne of cash, and your opinions on finance and money handling are far superior to everyone else. I call bullshit.

When you're a saver, there's a lot of good that can come with that, but there's also some bad. And when you're a spender, there's a ton of bad that comes with that, but there's also some good. Neither type of pattern is necessarily right or *wrong*. But as a society, we are quick to judge, painting savers in a positive light and spenders in a negative.

It's deeper than that. Money is an emotionally charged subject. In general, there are two types of personality traits: introverts and extroverts. Introverts are not automatically classified as superior to extroverts and the other way around. They are just different types of people. In the same way, we each have our own money personality. You wouldn't be judgmental of your partner for being an introvert or an extrovert because *that's who they are*. Their personality is a big part of the reason you fell in love in the first place. This concept can be applied directly to your significant other's money personality. Don't be quick to judge. Rather, pause to understand.

Typically, savers view the possession of money as the true goal. As a result, they become attached to their cash. They focus on building up their financial state and tie much of their success to their current financial status. That PFS growth is very important to them. This is a material financial strength because, as a society, we struggle with savings. On average, 42 percent of Americans have less than $1,000 in their savings account.[3] On the flip side, savers can sometimes be too attached to their money and can lose sight of the advantages a purchase might provide. This mentality might cost a saver more in the long run than their initial investment in the purchase.

Saver

Pros	Cons
Practices money mindfulness	Anxiety-driven behaviors around finances and timing
Debt averse	Does not adequately use debt as a means to grow
Risk averse	Apprehensive to invest money
Builds emergency funds	Does not properly invest in self to accelerate happiness and success

Spenders perceive money as a resource to help them achieve their goals, gain freedom, or acquire their desires. Whether that's investing in themselves, things, or other people, they typically subscribe to the idea of "It's spending and acquiring that drives my happiness, not the number in my account." When used strategically, I love this idea—that investment in the right assets or even oneself can actually increase a person's overall worth to others, their businesses, brand, image, and ultimately, to themselves. Obviously, there's a fine line here. Overspending can negatively affect a person's financial health, which is not where we want to be. But I want to debunk this myth that all spenders are undisciplined money managers, when in fact spenders have many positive attributes.

Spender

Pros	Cons
Tends to be giving and displays generosity	Typically follows a less detailed and disciplined money management plan
Sees value and can execute swiftly	May lack liquid cash flow
Values physical assets	More susceptible to slipping into debt
Invests heavily in personal brand	Overspends on depreciating assets or experiences

Maybe you're a spender or maybe you're a saver. Neither is right or wrong if properly managed. The key takeaway is to identify your money personality and then put parameters into place to adjust your spending accordingly. Everyone's solution will look different. *No cookie-cutter planning here.*

According to James Clear, author of *Atomic Habits*, it takes an average of sixty-six days to make a new habit automatic. So, if you're trying to change your money habits, don't get discouraged; be persistent. Remember, spending is a developed habit. Just like making your coffee in the morning. We don't think about our habits. They are automatic routines. It doesn't mean we can't fix these habits, but we do have to be aware and identify where we fall. We practice this all the time. If you're trying to get yourself in a better mental or physical state, you can't just snap your fingers and tomorrow your habits change. You have to understand the behaviors behind your developed habits and make a conscious effort to adjust.

In your gut, I would venture to guess you know your money personality.

Are you a saver?

Or a spender?

If you say you feel indifferent or both, I challenge you to dig deeper. Chances are you lean one way or the other.

Now I'm going to push you a step further.

	Yes	No
Are you worried more about what others think as opposed to what's best for you?	☐	☐
Did you inherit your spending habits from your family?	☐	☐
Were you in a previous or current relationship that influenced your money habits?	☐	☐
Are you quite literally trying to keep up with the Kardashians?	☐	☐

	Yes	No
Do you equate your value as a human to the balance in your bank account or the possessions you own?	☐	☐
Do you feel comfortable with your current saving and spending behaviors?	☐	☐

We can't fix tomorrow until we understand today. I'm a big believer in working on yourself before asking others, especially your partner, to evaluate their behaviors. And if your partner's money personality is different from yours, you need to educate yourself on their inherent behaviors, coming from a place of compassion and understanding.

Okay. That was a lot. How do you feel? Have you been able to identify some of your spending triggers? What about your money personality? If you're ready to reel in your spending or start spending, but you're not quite sure how, I have a great rule of thumb to help beef up your financial defense playbook.

THE 2 DOZEN JACK RULE

The b-word is tough. It makes my skin crawl when people scream b-u-d-g-e-t and then can't explain a simplified practice for someone to execute.

I think budgets have a negative connotation associated with them. They just aren't practical on a day-to-day basis for the masses. Want to know a secret? I don't use a budget. I'm an intentional spender who practices money mindfulness. Monthly, I spend one hour reviewing my inflows and outflows and set new goals for the following month.

So, given that I barely *budget, budget, budget,* how can I scream at you to do the same? If I asked you to sit down and put together a monthly budget, would you be excited to do it? I know I sure as hell wouldn't be. Putting together a spreadsheet of every single item that I *have* to pay for over the next month sounds like a form of cruel and unusual punishment. How can I possibly find the time to add up every Target or Amazon transaction down to the decimal? I'm not here to punish you. I'm here to reframe your idea of spending.

Everyone's spending and earnings will be different. Which is why one-size-fits-all solutions are ineffective. How can I prescribe one solution when you may be single, a DEWK (dual income with kids), a DINK (dual income, no kids), or even a DINK-WAD (dual income, no kids, with a dog)? Other than don't spend more than you earn and save the rest, there is no *perfect* answer when it comes to spending. A perfect answer would mean a cookie-cutter solution. In my experience, anyone in finance who offers cookie-cutter solutions isn't properly assessing your personal unique circumstances. My situation is different from yours, and yours might be different from your significant other's, and that's okay. What's important here is to be mindful with your money and to focus on your total cash inflows and total cash outflows. Let me explain.

If you have no idea what your spending *should* be, based on your income, I'm here to guide you. I created a rule of thumb to help you find your monthly, baseline spending figure, called the 2 Dozen Jack Rule. This guide is to make us cognizant of how we are spending and can be customized appropriately to fit your life!

Here's how it goes:

- Take your total gross income and divide it by 2.
  - Why? This gives us a conservative post-tax and post-deduction dollar amount that flows into your cash position annually. I'm conservatively estimating your net income will be about 50 percent of your gross income after paying federal, state, and local taxes, in

addition to any benefits, insurance, or retirement savings that would be automatically deducted from your paycheck. The beauty of being conservative with this estimation is that we may have a few extra bucks for saving trickle through, and we aren't even accounting for those extras!

- Take that number and divide it by a dozen, or 12.
  - Why? This gives us an after-tax and post-deduction dollar amount that flows into your cash position monthly.
- Now multiply that number by 0.90.
  - Why? This number will be the maximum amount you should target to spend in any given month! That means you can spend 90 percent of your after-tax monthly income on your expenses. Which means, I am asking you to save 10 percent! So, you may be asking yourself, *I get the 2, I get the dozen; why Jack?* Well, it's a fun way for this number to always remain top of mind . . . the 2 Dozen Jack Rule. For starters, a Jack in a deck of playing cards represents the value of 10. Just in case that won't have you remembering the 2 Dozen Jack Rule, I have a backup plan for you! Remember Jack Dawson from the movie *Titanic?* Well, he's a dime, he's 10/10. You want to save a Jack, or 10 percent. We are providing a 10 percent savings approach to after-tax and post-deduction monthly cash inflows into your cash position. We'll talk about what to do with that 10 percent in savings later, but with this equation, you can do the quick math to be mindful of where you stand.

That is the maximum amount you should target to spend in any given month. Just being aware of this number is a massive win. 2 DOZEN JACK! You got this!

Here's an example for someone who's gross income is $120,000:

- $120,000 / 2 = $60,000
- $60,000 / 12 = $5,000
- $5,000 x 0.90 = $4,500
- This individual should target to spend $4,500 or less in any given month. *That's for everything!* Rent, utilities, debt payments, dinners out, and so on. All the outflows to be targeted at $4,500 a month.

We really want our spending to fall within the magic, monthly number we just calculated. And if we do spend more than that number in any given month there needs to be a justification. Spending in that manner needs to be a literal outlier, like purchasing a car, a down payment on a house, or an emergency medical bill. It shouldn't be a month-to-month recurring behavior.

With every financial rule out there, there are exceptions, and those exceptions can be made. The importance here is that you understand where you are in relation to the 2 Dozen Jack Rule and can pinpoint specifically where you're off, understanding when and how future adjustments can be made.

Your spending will change based on where you live, your debt, or if you have dependents, but if you're lost on where you should be, follow the 2 Dozen Jack Rule. My number one goal is to make you aware of your outflows so we can identify and manage them moving forward.

VARIABLE AND FIXED EXPENSES

As a society, people have been keeping track of time since the Stone Age. Cavemen would track the length of a day or year based on the height of the sun and shape of the moon. Over time, these systems became regulated to form what we now call the Gregorian calendar. Believe it or not, the daily calendar sitting on your desk was actually developed in 1582.[4] Maybe not *your actual* calendar, but the concept of twelve months, fifty-two weeks, and 365 days in a regular year.

Who cares, right? Well, what if I told you that you can use *The Office* calendar your mom bought you for Christmas to predict the future. Let me explain.

Think about your own spending habits. Do you spend the same amount of money every single month without fail? Or is there some variance? For me, I know my most expensive month of the entire year is December. There's gift giving, travel to see family, expensive dinners out, which feels like almost every night during the holiday season. Not to mention I am usually flying back for at least one Bills game and booking flights and hotels based on the playoff schedule. I wouldn't trade these experiences for the world, but my spending habits during the holidays are much different from my spending habits in January or February.

Most Americans fall into this same category with winter being the most expensive season.[5] In fact, the average consumer spends nearly $1,500 on holiday gift giving every single year.[6] And that number is only rising with the impact of inflation.

I guess what I'm trying to say is that it's okay to spend. Being financially savvy doesn't mean you have to cheap out on things and people you love. It's actually the opposite. I *want* you to spend your money. But I want you to be proactive about it.

A reactive person will flow through the motions, marking an X on each day that passes by on the calendar without paying much attention. When the holidays roll around at the end of the year, this person is going to rack up a $1,500 bill on their credit card without a set plan on how to pay it off.

I'm going to let you in on a little secret: Christmas, Hanukkah, and Festivus occur around the same time every year. Don't react. Plan for it.

Americans spend the least in the beginning part of the year through the spring.[7] Use your calendar. Look at your year and the events you have coming up and plan for them accordingly. What actions can you take to prepare for the inevitable spending during the holidays or weekend trips with friends in the summer?

Actually, a ton of financially savvy people don't get tripped up by the inevitable. They take proactive steps. That can be as simple as setting up your checking account to automatically deduct $100 a pay period to your savings account. If you're paid biweekly, by December, you'll have $2,600 waiting for you to spend on the holidays. Set it and forget it until you need it.

Another strategy for proactive spending is to manage your future fixed and variable expenses. Every expenditure we have falls into one of two buckets: fixed or variable. **Fixed expenses** are typically monthly costs that remain constant for a set period of time. These are your not so fun bills, like rent, mortgage, insurance premiums, cell phone, utilities, loan payments, or taxes.[8] **Variable expenses** are costs that vary from month to month. For instance, dining out, travel, shopping, groceries, or unexpected costs like a car repair.[9]

When being proactive about our spending habits, fixed costs are the most difficult to change. In many circumstances, there's very little that can be done. If we sign an apartment lease for one year, we're locked into that rent price for the time being. The same can be said with student loans, mortgage, or car payments. One viable option is to refinance your loan or renegotiate the price of a fixed expense you're already locked in for by shopping competitors.

While you might not be tied to certain fixed expenses for a lifetime, in general, you're usually locked into lease, loan, or rent payments for a set period of time. Before jumping into a new fixed expense, make sure that cost doesn't push you over the 2 Dozen Jack Rule. And when you can, especially for home and auto loans, negotiate relentlessly.

Three Strategies to Manage Your Fixed Expenses

1. **Shop**—If you enjoy shopping, this is the best way to shop! Shop for things you are already paying for! For monthly fixed expenses like your rent, mortgage, cable, internet, phone, or insurance, *shop them*! Shop around these services every six months. Tell your vendors you are shopping; show them the offers you're given. You'll be surprised at how much room they have to adjust pricing, especially when it comes to retention. It's a red flag if you've been with the same provider for a long period of time. The time is now!
   - Tools to help: NerdWallet, The Points Guy, Credit Karma

2. **Eliminate**—According to Rocket Money, more than 80 percent of people have subscriptions they forgot about. And the average person has around twelve paid subscriptions! Identify all of your recurring costs by reviewing your monthly statement. Prioritize each of them top down, and eliminate at least the bottom 25 percent. It can be memberships, streaming services, subscriptions, and so on. Identify them and eliminate them.
   - Tools to help: Rocket Money

3. **Refinance**—Any asset that you own, in which you used credit to acquire, can be refinanced, and/or restructured.
   - First, understand specifically how your monthly expense is calculated. If you don't know, find out or *ask*. Buying something because of the monthly payment is *not* a reason to buy it. That is just a tool for salespeople to utilize to convince you to make the purchase.

- Second, see if there is an advantageous way to restructure and/or refinance the fixed expense. Consider refinancing your mortgage payment to a lower interest rate. Initially, refinancing will cost you some money up front, but you can roll the closing costs and other fees into your refinanced loan. Only restructure and refinance if the overall reduced costs from your new loan or rate will reduce the total amount paid from you to them.
- Tools that will provide calculators to see if it makes financial sense to restructure or refinance: Bankrate .com, LendingTree, SmartAsset, NerdWallet

Unlike fixed expenses, you have much more control over your monthly variable expenses. This is your moneymaker. Making slight adjustments in your spending behaviors and being mindful about those decisions will make the biggest impact on your bottom line.

There are outside forces that impact the cost of variable expenses, the major culprit in the last several years being inflation. Inflation coupled with increasing labor and supply costs means your dollar doesn't go as far. That's why it's crucial to be mindful of your money. The same dinner at the same restaurant is costing you almost 10 percent more than it was last year.[10] Am I saying you shouldn't go out to eat with your partner? Absolutely not! You should spend on experiences and things that bring you and your relationship joy.

But I'll challenge you with this question: In the past month, have you spent $100 or more on items you didn't really want or need? Maybe it was a drunken UberEats order or an impulsive Amazon purchase. And now, maybe you have buyer's remorse. It's all good. It happens to the best of us.

Moving forward, I simply want you to be more aware. Before making an unplanned purchase of $100 or more, ask yourself four questions.

FOUR QUESTIONS TO ASK BEFORE MAKING A VARIABLE EXPENSE

1. Will the item make me happier?
2. How is the value of the purchase one month from now compared to the spend? Worth it?
3. Does this purchase keep my monthly spending within the 2 Dozen Jack Rule?
4. Is this purchase adding an asset to my personal financial statement?

If you answered yes to all four questions, it's likely okay to pull the trigger and buy the damn thing! If you're feeling hesitant, sleep on it, and revisit the purchase tomorrow.

Being mindful of variable expenses and being proactive about future expenses are the easiest ways to keep extra money in your pocket. We may not be able to control every aspect of our fixed expenses or outside forces like inflation, but by developing intentional spending habits, we can grow our wealth without compromising on the things and people that matter most.

WHAT ARE YOUR ANNUAL EXPENSES?

When I was a banker, I worked with many CFOs across many industries and sizes. Some of my clients' companies earned $20 million in revenue annually, others $100 million, and a couple even earned over $1 billion. Regardless of size, the best CFOs were really good at **financial forecasting**. Forecasts are when you take the historical performance of the company, factor in the state of the economy, consider the business pipeline and the respective industry, put numbers to paper, and predict the company's financial future. The CFO presents the bank what the forecasted numbers will be in six months, one, two, three, and five years down the road. Some of the best CFOs of the largest companies in the United States are just brilliant at financial forecasting.

Remember from the last chapter, when I challenged you to be your own CFO? Well, I'm asking you to put that hat on again. You don't need to be the next CFO of Apple or Amazon, but you do need to be a good CFO for yourself. To achieve that, we need baseline numbers. One of those baseline figures is your annual spending. Don't skip this exercise, because, moving forward, I will ask you to pull this number.

I've talked your ear off about spending triggers, the psychology behind spending, identifying if you're a saver or spender, the 2 Dozen Jack Rule, and fixed versus variable expenses. We've gone through the who, what, where, and why behind your spending behaviors, but now it's time to answer the big question—*how much*?

Understanding your annual expenses is critical. We cannot course-correct until we have a baseline. Identifying spending behaviors and triggers is so important, but until we have the numbers in front of us, we're just ballparking our expenses. Don't play games with your money—get strategic! Why? Because *numbers don't lie*; they keep us honest!

You can find your total expenses one of two ways. The first way is by annualizing your monthly expenses. Break this list down into our two categories, fixed and variable. Once you have your total average monthly expenses, consider any outliers you have occurring in the next twelve months:

- Weddings
- Vacations
- Health-care costs
- Asset purchase, such as a car, home, property

Now add 15 percent to your annualized monthly expenses, including all outlier expenditures. We're adding this extra percentage to account for human error or an unforeseen emergency.

The second way to find your annual expenses is to log directly into your bank and credit card accounts. We have already listed all of those accounts in earlier chapters. Each bank is different, but typically, under accounts, you can view your monthly and annual spending. You also may be able to search by all of your "bank debits." Those will detail the list of transactions when funds were taken from your account. By looking at your spending this way, your bank will break down your transactions by categories, including bills, groceries, and entertainment. Using last year's annual spending data as a baseline, add 15 percent to your annualized expenses, including all outlier expenditures. This will account for inflation and any unforeseen emergencies.

Tip: When you go to statements and activities, often you can get a full-year report. If you can only get monthly statements, most banks will calculate your total withdrawals. They may even have an option to export your statement to Excel, which will make calculating this very easy. If your bank or credit company doesn't do either of these, maybe change; those are some dated resources. For the time being, though, you'll have to go through each transaction and add up your expenses.

Stop what you're doing! Start taking control of your financial freedom and go add up your expenses.

What are your annual expenses? Write it down and get it out in the open and start talking to your partner.

My Annual Expenses	**My Partner's Annual Expenses**

Golden Question, Yes or No.

Are you spending more than you earn _____?

Is your partner spending more than they earn _____?

Questions to start the conversation:

- Guess how much money I spent this year.
- What do you think was the most expensive purchase I made this year?
- How much do you think I have spent at _____ this past year?

Have fun with it, be vulnerable, and start to Talk Money!

Now maybe the numbers are higher than you anticipated, or maybe they're lower. Either way, it's okay. The important thing is now you know your baseline. There's no question mark, no guesswork—the number is in black and white. We really cannot move on until it's identified. This number will play a crucial part in the next chapter as we analyze how your joint expenses relate to your income and how to manage spending as a couple.

IT'S THE CLOSING BELL— IN THIS CHAPTER WE LEARNED

- Understanding your spending triggers and behaviors is crucial in improving your financial defense. Improving your defense will help you accumulate wealth as a couple.
- Almost everyone has a problem with overspending. The average American household spends 82 percent of their after-tax income. We can avoid being another statistic by practicing money mindfulness.

- Your monthly spending should not exceed your individualized, calculated figure, according to the 2 Dozen Jack Rule!
- Variable expenses are costs that vary from month to month, like entertainment, shopping, or an unexpected car repair.
- Fixed expenses are recurring monthly costs like rent, car payment, and utilities.
- We know the cost of big-ticket items, like how much we paid for our house or car, but very few people can answer how much they spend on annual expenses. Now that you know your annual expenses, how will you control your financial future?

6

HOW MUCH
DO YOU MAKE?

And What About Your
Expense-to-Income Ratio?

DING DING DING!!!
IT'S THE CHAPTER 6 OPENING BELL

- Tactics to Talk Money from one of the world's best negotiators: former FBI negotiator Chris Voss
- Finding the best joint spending system for you and your partner
- Calculating your expense-to-income ratio
- Breaking your bad money habits (we all have 'em . . .)
- Mindful money management
- Jason's credit card can-dos and how to find the card for you

When you have leverage in any situation, it can be used as a tool for power. A means to negotiate your desired outcome. Whether that leverage is used for the greater good is up to you.

Unfortunately, too many people leverage money in their personal lives with the wrong intention, devastating their relationships.

Chris Voss is arguably the world's best negotiator. During his twenty-four-year tenure with the Federal Bureau of Investigation, Voss was the lead international kidnapping negotiator. He's an expert at managing high-pressure, high-stakes scenarios like the kidnapping of journalist Jill Carroll in Iraq, the 1993 Chase Manhattan bank robbery, as well as multiple hostage situations in the Philippines, Colombia, Haiti, and other foreign nations. Today, Voss runs the Black Swan Group, a successful consulting agency that teaches businesses the art of negotiation.

According to Voss, most people think of leverage the wrong way. If someone has the upper hand over you, you can feel it. The Black Swan Group has a great quote: "Do you really think people are going to be happy working with you knowing that you're trying to take advantage of where they're sitting?"[1] This sort of leverage is not a solid foundation for negotiation; it's a breeding ground for animosity.

Leverage, when used properly, relies on trust, empathy, and a solution that works for both parties. How else would Voss be able to safely negotiate the release of multiple victims of international kidnappings and hostage situations? The bad guys committing these crimes aren't going to fold if they feel backed into a corner; they are going to retaliate in unimaginably horrific ways.

While you probably will never find yourself negotiating with a criminal over a cup of coffee, leverage is a very real facet of relationships. If one person is dangling their income or resources over their partner to get their way in other aspects of the relationship, that is extremely toxic behavior.

- "I make all the money so you owe me this!"
- "It's my house, so I get to decide how to train our dog!"
- "You make less than me, so your opinion doesn't matter as much!"

▶ "You're spending too much for someone who isn't making the money!"

Have you ever felt like your partner or past partner had the upper hand? Or maybe you had leverage over your partner? If so, was your conversation productive, or did it lead to a no-holds-barred argument?

There's a time and place for leverage, especially when negotiating your salary or cutting costs. But that mindset can go from very healthy and useful in the business world to poisonous in your personal life faster than a Bugatti. A word of advice: negotiation tactics in the boardroom don't translate well to the bedroom.

If one partner earns significantly more than their counterpart, it shouldn't be used as a stance of strength but rather a position of intention to begin the conversation regarding equitable financial systems. If you need help navigating these waters, don't fret. I'm going to break down three systems of spending to ensure you and your partner are approaching cash management as a team. If you'd like to hear more negotiating tactics and tricks from Chris Voss, scan the QR code to listen to my interview with him:

JOINT SPENDING SYSTEMS

It's impossible for me to know the exact nuances of your current earning or spending situation with your partner. Every relationship, from both a romantic and financial perspective, is unique to you, like a fingerprint. That being said, it's likely you fall into one of three buckets as it relates to earnings. As you read through these systems, please keep in mind that you will always have your own fingerprint and adjust these generalizations to fit your unique situation.

Earnings Bucket One: Same Wavelength: One partner doesn't need to be paying for everything when it comes to joint expenses. With partners that earn the same amount of income within a 15 percent differential of each other, I recommend a fifty-fifty approach, unless of course there's an underlying circumstance, like a large debt. If you open a joint account, you and your partner will contribute the same amount every pay period to that account, both of you will have equal access, and you will mutually agree on a set of rules for these funds. This account could be used for rent, mortgage, groceries, vacations, dining, utilities, whatever fits your partnership. By contributing the same amount, there is no leverage in your relationship—you're on the same wavelength.

If you have followed the rules of this book so far, you have already established visibility to one another's financial picture. Thus, the same-wavelength approach will solve for joint spending.

Earnings Bucket Two: Teeter-Totter: Both partners are working, but there is more than a 15 percent differential in income. Imagine this as a teeter-totter on a playground—the earnings are out of balance. If you fall into this category, use the following equation:

How Much Will You Contribute to the Joint Account

Partner A gross income + Partner B gross income
= total joint income

Partner A gross income / total joint income
= pro rata percent

Partner B gross income / total joint income
= pro rata percent

Let's put this equation to the test. Imagine partner A makes $100,000 annually and partner B makes $60,000. Their total joint income is $160,000. Partner A takes their gross income of $100,000 and divides it by $160,000. Partner A's pro rata percentage is 62.5 percent. Partner B does the same thing, dividing their gross income of $60,000 by $160,000. Partner B's pro rata percentage is 37.5 percent. The pro rata percentage is a proportional amount based on each partner's income. It doesn't feel equitable for each partner to contribute the same dollar amount when partner A is earning $40,000 more annually.

When creating a joint account, set similar spending rules as the same-wavelength approach and allow both parties to have equal access, but instead of matching each other's contribution dollar for dollar, use the pro rata percentage. For instance, if you and your partner decide you want to contribute a joint total of $1,000 per month to your joint account, partner A would use their percentage of 62.5 percent, contributing $625, and partner B would contribute their percentage of 37.5 percent, or $375. Now leverage cannot be abused for joint spending as both partners are contributing the same proportion of their income.

Earnings Bucket Three: Anchor Approach: One partner works and supports the family, and the other partner does not work or is a stay-at-home partner (SAHP). Envision this system as an anchor. The person staying at home is the anchor, allowing the partner earning income the flexibility to work by taking care of the home, the pets, the kids, the aging parents, and so on. The partner working wouldn't be able to have the same career success without the other partner staying at home. The SAHP is the anchor.

That said, this scenario is the most susceptible to leverage, or power abuse. If one partner is making 100 percent of the income and the other is making 0 percent, the person without any inflows may feel inadequate. We need to kick that mentality to the curb and bring the financial partnership to a level playing field. Just because the SAHP isn't a corporate warrior does not mean they aren't working. Their workday doesn't end at 5:00 p.m.—it's an all-consuming, full-time job that deserves respect and appreciation. To aid this process, my suggestion is to assign dollars and cents to all the work, effort, and time the SAHP provides—a massive value to the family. Break down a list of items you take care of and find the national average. These items can include housecleaning, childcare, pet care, caring for aging parents or a sick family member, and so on. Whatever value you provide, attach a dollar amount to that service. This will show how much money you're saving the family, while supporting your partner who provides the income, balancing the financial partnership and dissipating leverage.

Since money is coming in from only one partner, there needs to be a set agreement in place. Both partners need to be fully aligned and compromise with how much money can be spent and on what items. Recognize you are in a joint partnership and that both partners are bringing the same value in different forms. Meet in the middle, throw leverage aside, and create a financial plan that you both follow religiously.

WHAT'S YOUR EXPENSE-TO-INCOME RATIO?

Now that we understand how to manage your joint expenses, if you are an income earner, we need to understand your individual expenses as they relate to your income. Understanding your individual expenses will put you in a position to better manage your joint expenses with your partner.

So far, you've already discussed your credit score, your personal financial statement, money mindfulness, the 2 Dozen Jack Rule, and joint expenses with your partner. Now it's time to take the conversation a step further and get candid about your expense-to-income ratio.

Calculating Your Expense-to-Income Ratio

Step 1: Find Your Total Expenses: Good news! You already calculated your annual expenses in the last chapter. Refer back to page 97 to find that number.

Step 2: Find Your Annual Net Income: If you're a W-2 employee, your paycheck will list your gross income, which is your total income before taxes and benefits are deducted. Your net income is your after-tax total take-home pay. For the purpose of finding your expense-to-income ratio, you will only need your annual net income.

If you have any side gigs or other sources of income, make sure you include those additional after-tax dollars to your annual net income.

Step 3: Doing the Math: To calculate your ratio, simply divide your expenses by income and multiply by 100 to find the percentage.

For example, if your total annual expenses are $50,000 and your net income is 70,000, your equation will look like this:

$$\$50,000 \div \$70,000 = 0.71 \times 100 = 71 \text{ percent}$$

A percentage to aim for is 70–75 percent. This means you are saving or investing 25–30 percent of your total net income. This is the low hazard zone. This is amazing! If your ratio is close to 80–95 percent, we are in the medium hazard zone, and anything above 95 percent, we are in the high hazard zone. If you're in the medium or high hazard zone, one of two things needs to happen: increase your inflows or decrease your outflows. These adjustments can be directly related to your money habits, which we will discuss shortly.

Expense-to-Income Ratio Warning Flags

- ▶ High Hazard: A ratio of 95 percent or greater
- ▶ Medium Hazard: A ratio between 80 and 95 percent
- ▶ Low Hazard: A ratio of 75 percent or lower

If your expense-to-income ratio, or your partner's ratio, is more than our 70–75 percent benchmark, that's okay! Like we discussed earlier, we can't change our habits and routines until we identify our baseline. If your ratio is more favorable than your partner's or vice versa, there is no shame. Rather than be defensive or accusatory, approach the conversation with an open mind and an open heart. The important thing is to find your ratio, discuss the results with your partner, and put together an action plan to improve the ratio. Don't dwell on the number. Instead, change your psychology as it relates to money and spending. Get comfortable with the uncomfortable. This will not only benefit you but also your significant other as you build and grow your life together.

My Annual Expenses	**My Partner's Annual Expenses**
My Annual Income	**My Partner's Annual Income**
My Expense/Income Ratio	**My Partner's Expense/Income Ratio**

Our Joint Expense/Income Ratio

BREAKING YOUR BAD MONEY HABITS
(TWO METHODS)

Do you and your partner feel like you're on the spending struggle bus? Have no fear! There are two surefire ways to help couples break their bad money habits. If this is the first time you're dipping your toes into the financial waters, I recommend using the rookie method. It's a quick, straightforward strategy to identify what, where, and how frequently you and your partner are spending. By identifying the basics, we can be more mindful of these money habits for the future. If you have a financial foundation, I recommend the pro method. Here we identify your baseline financial health score and create a custom solution for you to improve that baseline based on your spending routines.

Rookie Method: There are 24 hours in a day, on average 30.44 days in a month, and approximately 730 hours in a month. All I'm asking for is one hour of your entire month. And don't tell me you don't have it to spare. We both know that's bullshit at its most pristine. Think of all the mindless hours in your month you could easily subtract sixty minutes from without noticing. All that mindless scrolling, all those hours logged hate-watching that show you never really liked in the first place. I'm only asking you to trade out one. That's literally 0.1369 percent of your time for the month. That's a pretty attainable commitment, wouldn't you agree? All right, let's go. Once a month, I want you to go old school. Print out your bank statements like it's 1993 and go over every line-by-line transaction with your partner. When you actually have the bank statement in your hands, you're more aware. The intangible becomes more tangible. You can hold it, see it, make notes, and compare it to the previous month. You become more mindful of your basic inflows and outflows. When you're going through each line item, I want you to grade each transaction Red, Yellow, Green:

Red: I want it, don't need it, can go without it.

Yellow: I want it, don't need it, would like to have it.

Green: I want it, I need it, can't live without it.

Each cash outflow needs to be assigned an R, Y, or G. The process of forcing yourself to prioritize these expenditures will allow you to subconsciously improve spending habits in the coming months! Now, I want you to ask yourself two questions:

1. What is the total amount of **cash inflow** for the month?
2. What is the total amount of **cash outflow** for the month?

Once you identify the spending areas you may need to tweak, I want you to ask your partner the same. "Where do you think I can improve?" Just do me a solid and make sure to keep it finance focused, or you might be awakening a beast only a seasoned therapist and vat of vodka can help you tame. If you notice a particular spending habit you're struggling with, ask your partner for support. Lean on each other. Understand your spending triggers. Make a strategic plan to reduce your outflows so you can increase your monthly cash flow. By opening up and communicating with each other, your relationship will be so much stronger.

Pro Method: Every year, you get a physical or have bloodwork taken so you can find your health baseline. Depending on the results of that appointment, you may have to make changes to your daily routines, like limiting your red meat or sodium intake. It's a little adjustment that will make a big impact on the quality and longevity of your life. It's not a big deal; it's just your new normal. But for some reason, we don't take this same approach with our finances. Here are the solutions that will put you and your partner in a position to see your baseline number so you can make the appropriate adjustments to your lifestyle.

To discover your baseline, you need to use technology to your advantage. Specifically, by using an app that syncs your bank accounts, bills, subscription services, and more, organizing all of your expenditures in one place. This will give you a bird's-eye view of where your money is really going . . . and more importantly, how much! One tool I'd recommend is Rocket Money. It uses multi-factor authentication and the latest secure technology to ensure your personal and financial data is kept safe.

No matter which financial management app you decide to use, I urge you to take advantage of two features:

1. Automatic bill pay: This will guarantee you are never late on all the bills you *have* to pay. If you want to boost your credit score, set these bills to automatically be paid in full every month.
2. Automatic savings transfer: Remember the 10 percent savings we discussed during the 2 Dozen Jack Rule? Using your financial management app, automatically set up 10 percent of your paycheck to go to a savings or investment account. This set-it-and-forget-it mentality is an easy way to build your wealth!

Improving your financial health doesn't have to be tedious. Instead, set yourself up for success by using technology and automation to your advantage. Implementing those positive changes today will pay dividends years from now. Those extra dollars you save can be allocated in a myriad of ways: investments, retirement, or simply spending on things you *want*. Let's be honest, spending on something you've had your eye on for a long time is extremely rewarding, but we can't experience that joy unless we are mindful of our everyday expenses.

NEVER OVERPAY FOR TOOTHPASTE AGAIN— MINDFUL SPENDING!

Ugh, this story of my spending was hard to put in the book. It may be perceived as unrelatable, somewhat off-putting and a bit douchey. But this is the risk of Talking Money, and I'm choosing to silence the voices telling me not to Talk Money. This is an example to showcase how sometimes crazy spending can actually provide an ROI, if you're tactful. Could you imagine someone spending $18,200 on a watch? Would you say that person is an overspender? Or maybe that they're reckless with their money? Probably.

What if I told you that person was me?

We're so quick to judge. In relationships and in life. But behind the potentially shocking amount I spent on this watch was a mindful money decision. One that I didn't take lightly or rush into. Let me walk you through the process.

Before I get into the numbers behind the spending decision, I want to talk about my why. My entire life I've wanted to own one specific luxury item, a Rolex! I'm a big watch guy, and Rolex is the premier watch manufacturer in the world. They create stunning pieces, and it's always been my goal to be able to afford one. Aside from a beautiful product, it's also a conversation starter. If you're at a networking event and a watch collector notices your time-piece, it could be an introduction that leads to potential business opportunities. Crazy and weird to think about, but trust me, it happens!

Before jumping into the dollars and cents, it's important to note that this was *my* purchase. This wasn't a gift; there were no discounts or deals. Beyond the emotional piece of my spending decision, I had to do some research to justify making this exorbitant purchase. The watch I decided to buy was a 42mm 18K yellow gold and steel black dial Sky-Dweller. The retail price was $18,200. This piece is hard to come by because of the lack of available supply and increased Rolex and Sky-Dweller demand. I looked at prices for this same watch on the secondary market, and it was reselling for $27,000. Rolex is one of the few luxury brands in which the resell market sells for more than the retail price at official Rolex jewelers. Imagine you buy a car at the dealership, except when you drive off the dealership property the car's value increases substantially! This new watch is an appreciating asset, and at the time of this writing it would resell at approximately 36 percent more than what I purchased it for. My intention is not to resell this watch. In fact, if I get caught reselling it, the Rolex dealer will likely take me off their "list" and will not offer me watches to purchase anymore through their official jewelers. It's wild, but trust me, it's a whole thing. But there are no rules against doing so, and many do it daily. That said, it's a reassuring sort of safety net to know that if I needed to, I could resell the Rolex at a profit.

At the same time I was making these purchases, I also signed up for a Hilton Honors Amex credit card that provided hotel points. Because I travel so frequently, it made sense to have a credit card that gave me rewards. Don't worry, readers, we're going to get to how to pick out the right credit card for you because not all cards are created equal in relation to rewards. Strategically, I charged $18,200 plus tax ($19,474) on my Hilton Honors Amex. This purchase unlocked 150,000 welcome rewards points. Then I received 58,422 points for the actual purchase, and then I hit my annual purchases necessary to get a few free nights' stay at any Hilton in the world. According to The Points Guy, a credible website that analyzes travel and rewards points, on this specific credit card the value is 0.6 cents per acquired point.[2] So, $0.006 x 208,422 points = $1,250.53 of added value in points. So just by using my credit cards strategically, I walked away with more than $1,200 in reward points, plus a few nights' stay, plus an appreciating asset I have always wanted that could be liquidated at the drop of a dime. And most importantly, I budgeted and saved so that the entire balance was paid off immediately. The current market value of this timepiece can be added to the Other Assets section of my PFS and, of course, I have insured the asset, which will be discussed in greater detail in later chapters! The objective of this story is to dispel the immediate judgment we may feel when our significant other tells us about a big purchase they're entertaining. Before jumping down your partner's throat, stop and ask how they're thinking through the purchase. Ask thoughtful questions instead of making assumptions. Being mindful of your spending isn't exclusive to big purchases. I would make the argument that we need to be *more* conscious of regular spending. Process and decision-making on spending is critical because these habits will last a lifetime.

If you listen to my podcast, *Trading Secrets*, you might remember my interview with TikTok star Kiersti Torok (@torok.coupon .hunter). She has more than 2.5 million faithful followers who look to her for the latest tips and tricks on savings and deals for everyday items. Both Kiersti and I have one major thing in common: money mindfulness.

Her tagline is that you should never, ever, under any circumstance pay full price for toothpaste. The idea behind this is that we have to save money on things we *need* so we can spend money on things we *want*. One of the best ways to do this is to take advantage of retail stores' coupons.

Forget about granny hunched over the kitchen table wielding scissors like a samurai sword against Sunday's paper. The world has evolved. In this digital age, retailers are moving away from physical coupons and items marked down in the store. Kiersti's secret: download the store's app.

Say you do the majority of your errand shopping at Target. They have a free app called Target Circle. I want you to download it. All major retailers have their own app, and baked within the app are hundreds of dollars of savings. You just have to take five minutes.

It's a Thursday afternoon and you're doing your weekly shopping at Target. You've already walked around the store for an hour. Sip the coffee you bought at Starbucks on the way in and take five minutes. Open up the Circle app and scan the items in your cart (the scanner will be on the home page of the app). The app will automatically let you know if any coupons apply to the items in your cart. Any money you save will be after tax, which is valued one and a half times higher than pretax money. Once you're in the checkout line, hand your phone to the cashier to apply the coupons and go on your merry way.

Do this every time you're at the store and save a few hundred bucks a month. It's very reasonable to assume you can save $5,000 a year using Kiersti's coupon strategy. That's after-tax money. If you multiply that number by one and a half, that's like adding $7,500 to your annual gross income. All because you took five minutes. Now you can use those dollars on things and experiences that matter most, rather than overspending on necessities, like toothpaste.

FINDING THE RIGHT
CREDIT CARD FOR *YOU*

You've been thinking about it. Maybe you're in a position to get a new credit card, or even your first card. Perhaps you saw a newer, shinier card that provides all the rewards. Before you pull the trigger, you need to stop and ask yourself why.

You know me, I like to keep things simple and fun. From what I've noticed, if you're looking to get a new credit card, you'll typically fit into one of three categories.

Category	You	Your Want	Your Why
Minnow	You're a minnow in the ocean. You're new to the credit card game.	You're looking into applying for your first credit card.	You want to start establishing credit, but you're not sure where to start.
Fish	You're swimming with the school of fish. You have good credit, good income, but you're looking to step up your credit card game.	You're looking to refinance old credit card debt with a 0 percent interest rate card, or you want to take advantage of a new card's introductory offer.	You're not a minnow anymore. You want to start taking advantage of the rewards and benefits some credit cards have to offer.
Shark	You're the king of the ocean. You have multiple credit cards or you're a big spender, and you want to get the most bang for your buck in terms of rewards points. You pay your card in full every month.	You want a new card that provides perks based on the lifestyle you're already living. You don't bite at the first credit card offer you see. You're lurking in the water, waiting for the best offer.	You recognize most of your spending is coming from restaurants, gas stations, or travel. You want to be a strategic spender and are looking for a card that rewards your habits.

Once you identify which category you fall into, what you want out of your new credit card, and why, it's time to put the pedal to the metal. I'm gonna teach you how to pick the right card for you, as well as provide practical advice and common credit card sand traps to avoid. Let's break down each individual strategy to help achieve your desired why.

Minnow: Before you open your first credit card, you need to recognize that a credit card isn't free money. When you swipe that card, you're taking responsibility for whatever item you're purchasing, and if you don't, you'll be charged a hefty interest rate down the road. And kicking the can will not work! They will find you, they likely will get paid, and you will have repercussions for misusing. So develop a healthy relationship with your credit card early on so you don't have to course-correct later. There are many types of cards you can apply for, if you don't have credit history:

- Student credit card—If you're between the ages of eighteen and twenty-one, you can apply for a student credit card. In order for your application to be approved, you'll usually have to show some form of income, like a part-time job.
- Secured credit card—We already discussed this one in the credit chapter. Refresher: You provide an up-front deposit (say, $500) and that is your total credit card limit. If you can't pay back the balance, no harm, no foul, the bank will just use your deposit to pay off your debt.
- Cards that allow a cosigner—The credit card will be in your name, but you'll need a friend or relative with credit history to act as a cosigner. If you can't foot the bill, your cosigner will be on the hook, so be cautious.[3]

A good resource for all things credit card related, especially as it pertains to first-time, entry-level cards, is The Points Guy. On his website (https://thepointsguy.com/credit-cards/first/) he breaks down a list of the top five credit cards for beginners with no credit history. When analyzing this list, pay attention to the interest rate, annual fee, and penalties.

Fish: At this point, you already have an established credit history. Now you want to make the most of your card. There are two really good strategies to use if you're in this boat: introductory offers and refinance opportunities.

Here's what you have to understand: credit card companies want your business. But through marketing, it's really expensive for these companies to acquire new clients. So what do they do to encourage customers to move their business? They provide introductory offers. It's essentially a temporary 0 percent interest rate that lasts anywhere from six to twenty-four months to incentivize consumers to open an account and make purchases. Spenders who aren't mindful with their money will swipe this new card on everyday items without giving it a second thought. This is where I want you to be strategic.

I financed my entire MBA on a 0 percent introductory credit card offer. I was in my midtwenties and had a full-time job that paid roughly $105,000. My MBA program was really expensive, just under six figures. And no, I don't think it was worth it. Anyway, every quarter, I had an $8,000–$9,000 tuition payment due. Instead of taking out a student loan, I opened up a new credit card that offered a 0 percent rate for twenty-four months. Every time a tuition payment was due, I would charge it to the card. I set up a strict budget for myself, making sure to pay off the total credit card balance by the time the 0 percent offer expired. This period of my life really sucked. I couldn't afford to go out to bars or spend a ton of money at restaurants. I was the "no" man. I couldn't meet you for drinks, lunch, dinner, or even breakfast at the cheap diner. My PFS was ugly, and I knew it would require massive life adjustments for the short term to make the long term better. Call it my ramen noodle and Busch Light phase! I had to decrease my variable expenses in order to increase my excess cash flow, ensuring I didn't fall into massive credit card debt.

I have friends who have used this same 0 percent introductory offer strategy to finance their entire wedding. The couple charged everything to the card, they put together a payment plan, and made sure the card was paid off by the expiration of the offer. That doesn't mean they went over budget; it just means they used strategic financing to reduce any cash flow issues. Do you have a big purchase on the horizon that could benefit from this financing strategy? If using this tactic, pay close attention to the length of the introductory period and any fees associated with the card.

Another way to step up your credit card game is to refinance old credit card debt. You can bring over old debt to a new credit card that has a lower interest rate. If your current credit card balance is $3,000 and you're paying a 28 percent interest rate, that's no good. Over a two-year period, you'd pay over $950 in interest alone! That's one-third of the damn balance! Or you could save yourself money and transfer the balance to a new credit card that offers a 0 percent interest transfer. Again, pay close attention to the length of the introductory offer and put together a plan to guarantee you pay off the balance by the time the offer expires. Also, keep an eye out for transfer fees.

Resource for 0 percent interest cards: https://wallethub.com /credit-cards/0-apr/.

Shark: Oh, you fancy, huh? You're the big spender in the ocean. You know what you're doing, but you wanna add a little finesse to your credit card game. Don't worry, I got you. There are three main areas that provide benefits; you just have to decide what's best for you.

Cash back: When you examined your annual expenses in the previous chapter, did you find you were spending most in a certain category? Maybe it's restaurants, groceries, gas stations, or entertainment. Whatever the area, hunt for cards with the highest percentage of cashback for your specific spending. You literally will get money back for your everyday expenditures.

Travel and leisure: How much are you spending on travel, hotel, and airfare? If you're a jet-setter like me, you'll like that many credit cards offer travel points that equate to benefits. As I've mentioned before, The Points Guy provides detailed insight not only on the best credit card offers but also the specific value of rewards points. You can put in an estimation of how many airline miles you will get from a specific card, similar to my Rolex example, helping you understand each card's benefits and how they fit into your lifestyle. An important disclaimer: most of these credit cards will have an annual fee. You need to determine whether the rewards you receive will bring a value greater than the annual fee.

Here's a real-life example for you. At the time this book was written, the American Express Platinum Card was offering eighty thousand welcome rewards points (worth two cents per point; thanks, Points Guy), in addition to multiple store credits, for one year. The annual fee for this card is no joke at $695. I did the math to see if the benefits outweigh the hefty annual fee.[4]

American Platinum Consideration

Welcome Offer	80,000	0.02	$1,600.00
Airline Credit			$200.00
Hotel Credit			$200.00
Walmart Credit			$155.00
Media Subscription Credit			$240.00
Uber Cash			$200.00
Saks 5th Avenue Credit			$100.00
Equinox Credit			$300.00
TSA Precheck and Clear Credit			$189.00
Total Tangible Value			$3,184.00
Annual Fee			$695.00
First-Year Value			$2,489.00

So the total tangible value of the Amex Platinum card is $3,184, less the annual fee of $695, bringing us to a total benefit of $2,489. It's a no-brainer. The rewards from the first-year welcome offer are three and a half times the annual fee. Next year, when the welcome offer is gone, we would have to analyze if our spending and rewards points can justify the fee. A word to the wise: don't jump on the first welcome offer you find. Shop around because these offers fluctuate quite a bit based on timing and location.

Niche: If you spend a ton at a specific store or brand, you might consider a niche credit card. Maybe you're a die-hard Buffalo Bills fan (sound familiar?) and you spend a ton of money on NFL merchandise and game-day tickets. If that's the case, you should consider the NFL Extra Points Card so you can earn 3 percent back on those purchases.[5] Or if you're really into DIY projects, maybe you should consider the Home Depot card to receive discounts on purchases. Whatever the store, analyze if those niches make sense for your spending. Don't just sign up for a store's credit card to earn a onetime 20 percent discount off your purchase. Be strategic and understand your why.

IT'S THE CLOSING BELL— HERE'S WHAT WE LEARNED

- If one partner earns significantly more than their counterpart, it shouldn't be used as leverage. Ditch the mentality of keeping score—you're on the same team. Instead, begin the conversation regarding equitable financial systems to benefit your partnership.
- Three joint spending systems:
  - Same Wavelength—you and your partner earn the same within a 15 percent differential.
  - Teeter-Totter—there is greater than 15 percent differential between your incomes. Reference the pro rata equation to level the playing field.
  - Anchor Approach—one partner makes the majority of the income. How to avoid being a victim of leverage or power abuse.

- Breaking your bad money habits. We reviewed methods to reduce your spending whether you're a rookie or a pro.
  - Bottom line: Increase your cash inflow and decrease your cash outflow.
- Calculating your expense-to-income ratio:
  - Divide your total annual expenses by your total net income and multiply by 100.
  - Try to aim for the 70–75 percent zone.
- Deep dive into my $18,200 purchase of my Rolex watch and how I used credit card rewards to my advantage.
  - I wouldn't have been able to make this purchase without money mindfulness.
  - TikTok star and expert couponer Kiersti Torok teaches us how to save thousands of dollars on items we need (like toothpaste) so we can spend extravagantly on items we want.
- How to find the right credit card for you, whether you're a minnow, fish, or shark.

7

WHAT IS YOUR
DEBT-TO-INCOME RATIO?

Don't Let Loans Get in the Way of Love

DING DING DING!!!
IT'S THE CHAPTER 7 OPENING BELL

- How to stop the bleeding—everyone has debt; we must learn to manage it!
- $25,000 in rolling credit card debt is costing you more than $115,000 in interest
- Get your current liabilities out in the open
- How to attack the living hell out of your current debt
- Learn from Netflix's Cecilie Fjellhøy how the Tinder Swindler swindled her!
- Understanding your debt-to-income ratio

It's Sunday afternoon. The Buffalo Bills are getting ready to play their divisional rivals the Miami Dolphins. I'm blasting "Shout" by the Isley Brothers while making lunch in the kitchen. I'm fired up! It's gonna be a great day.

As I'm cutting up celery to go with my perfectly hot, extra crispy wings, the knife slips, and I slice my hand. There's a huge gash, right along my palm.

Shit! In a flash, my countertop looks like a scene out of a Tarantino film. Blood everywhere.

I snatch a towel and put pressure on the wound. The cut's deep enough and wide enough that I know stitches are in my future. I get the keys, keep pressure on, and rush to the nearest urgent care. And even though every fiber of my Bills-lovin'-being wants nothing more than wings and a game right now, thanks to this little unscheduled intermission, the rest of my world screeches to a halt. All that matters now is stopping the bleeding, avoiding infection, and resolving this misstep ASAP.

Have you ever been in a situation like this? Whether it was a broken bone, a flat tire, a horrific toothache, a burst pipe in your house, a sick kid or pet, something so pressing that you have an immediate need to address the pain point. Everything else in your life gets pushed to the back burner until you resolve the issue.

Now, have you ever taken this same urgency with your finances? Moreover, do you know how to recognize if you're in financial distress that may require immediate attention, as immediate as a gash in your hand? As a society, we're constantly fed information, resources, and products that align with improving our physical and mental health. This is fantastic and something I totally support. But we tend to ignore a big piece to that wellness puzzle: our financial health. If we allow debt to accumulate, roll over, and run our lives, that is a *huge* stressor. It can cause major anxiety, which affects our overall health and well-being. Even worse, the system is set up in a way that allows us to ignore the bleeding. It's almost like living in a world in which you slice your finger but don't bleed. Bizarre, but hear me out.

Part of the financial deception, part of the strategy from some of the banking institutions, is to not let you see the cut and feel the pain. Let me explain. If you or your partner have revolving credit card debt, which is when you pay only the minimum balance from month to month, your bank likely isn't going to say a peep. Why? Because they're making an assload of money off the interest you're accumulating while you're technically paying on time. Essentially, by paying only the minimum balance, you're putting a baby Band-Aid on a wound that needs stitches. But the financial institutions don't care. They're not going to bring this to your attention. They're not going to call you up and say, "Hey, you might want to pay off your current balance before you keep charging your credit card." As long as you keep making the minimum payment, you're the bank's cash cow. The urgency here won't come from the blood pouring out, or the pain of the cut; it will only come from you seeing the bigger picture of what the debt you are carrying is really costing you.

RECOGNIZE THE BLEEDING

There's a certain shame and blame associated with the word *debt*. Mainly, because we don't talk about how common it is or how to manage it. So, instead of trying to fix our situation, we sweep it under the rug. Check your shame at the door because you're not as alone as you think. In the United States there is

- $10.93 trillion in credit card debt,
- $1.58 trillion in student loan debt,
- $11.93 trillion in mortgage debt, and
- $96,371 in average debt per American.[1]

For the sake of your financial future, security, freedom, and growth, we need to give these liabilities the same level of attention as the cut on your hand. We need to stop throwing the notices away, ignoring the bills, and deleting the email reminders. We can't just ignore the things we don't like. The days of not-so-stealthily slipping your broccoli to the dog under the table are long gone. You weren't fooling your parents then, and you're not fooling yourself now. We can't hide from our fears. I want you to accept your debt. We cannot change unless we accept the reality of the situation. And according to the statistics, the reality is, we *all* have debt.

The path of least resistance is to ignore something that we feel insecure about or have fear over. To tiptoe around our anxieties. For me, one nemesis comes to mind: needles. Those tiny stainless steel fuckers have been the bane of my existence since I was knee high. I hate 'em. And look, I get it, no one out there is crocheting hypodermics on pillows. We all hate them. Novocain at the dentist, bloodwork at our annual physical, it all sucks. But trust me when I say, my dislike for those thin little tormentors was borderline unhinged. So how did I handle it? By ignoring it, of course. I literally didn't go to the doctor for five years. If there was even a sliver of the possibility that a needle might make a cameo, my ass was out! Then once I hit my mid- to late-twenties, I knew I had to grow up. I couldn't keep avoiding my regular checkups. In order to get over my phobia, I sought help from a psychiatrist—borderline unhinged, remember?

My doctor started a process called exposure therapy. Instead of "show me the money," it was "show me the needles." Not really, but you get it. Instead of ignoring and avoiding phobias, which temporarily reduces anxiety but still maintains the fear, exposure therapy is designed to reduce those irrational feelings by gradually exposing the patient to various aspects of their fear. After a certain amount of exposure, your brain becomes adaptable, and your phobia starts to dissipate.[2] This helped immensely with my fear of needles.

When it comes to debt management, many people are doing the same thing I did with needles and the doctor. They just ignore the issue. Statements and notices get stuffed in a drawer that we never open again. The problem is, the system benefits from your fear. All the interest you're allowing to pile up is taking your hard-earned money and putting it in the pockets of the financial institutions.

Ignoring the problem is a temporary fix that will only end up harming you. And only you.

Just like my psychiatrist used exposure therapy to help my fear of needles, I want you to use this approach with your liabilities. Open up the statements and notices from the bank you've been ignoring. Look at your outstanding balances. Familiarize yourself with the numbers.

Now stop.

Leave the statements out where you can see them, your kitchen table, desk, your bathroom sink, it doesn't matter. Just don't put them away where they can be easily ignored.

Before getting into any technical bullshit with crunching numbers, spreadsheets, and ratios, we need to get comfortable with our current liabilities. Debt is okay, but we have to jump on top of it. If we don't jump on top of it, it's like gashing your hand and not stopping the bleeding. Today, we get comfortable with the fact that all of us need some sort of help, whether it's a Band-Aid, stitch, or reconstructive surgery. We're all bleeding financially to some degree. And if we know our partner is struggling with debt, not helping them is like watching them bleed out. Today we stop the bleeding.

JASON'S RELATIONSHIP RULES

1. At all costs avoid providing your partner a loan, especially if you're not married.
2. If you don't listen to rule number one, have a legal contract in place for that loan.
3. And make sure you have some form of collateral pledged for any lending you do.

This may seem overprotective, unreasonable, and overbearing. And it is, because, historically, intercouple loans prior to marriage without contracts have a high failure rate.

UNDERSTANDING YOUR LIABILITIES

How are you feeling? Are you getting comfortable with your debt? Do you want to stick it to the banks, who are benefiting from your lack of action? Are you ready to stop the bleeding with your partner? I want you to *want* to take control of your financial future. Because if you feel passionately about something, it shows. Your success rate will be much higher than if you feel obligated to check another box off the to-do list. This is your future—get excited about taking ownership!

If you're ready to take the next step, I want to make something crystal clear: understand how much debt you have, but do not obsess over the dollar amount. That might sound counterintuitive coming from a numbers guy, but let me ask you this question: Person A has $500,000 in debt and Person B has $25,000 in debt. Do you have enough information to know who's in a better position with managing their liabilities? Specifically, who has an action plan in place for tackling their debt? The answer is *no*.

The person with the higher debt balance isn't automatically worse off. In fact, Person A and Person B are real people I know. Person A is a surgeon. That $500,000 in debt they have incurred is all student loans. Without those loans, Person A would not be in a position to make their current salary of seven figures. As a result, they have accelerated their paydown and will pay off their debt in less than seven years. Person A will be a multimillionaire in the blink of an eye, and they will likely be practicing for decades to come. I would classify this as **good debt**. Debt that you take out that has a high probability of adding value or increasing your net worth is debt that I support. Another example would be a residential mortgage loan: they are generally considered good debt because historical returns suggest that the debt will be used to support the financing of an asset that will appreciate and grow in value more than the cost of the loan.

On the flip side, Person B has $25,000 in revolving credit card debt. This individual is paying 28 percent in interest. If Person B decides to pay off this balance in 240 months, which is the equivalent of twenty years, the monthly payment would be $585. Over that twenty years, Person B will pay $25,000 in principal and $115,554 in interest.[3] *Ouch!* But keep in mind, Person B is not an anomaly: 51 percent of baby boomers and millennials with credit card debt say that day-to-day expenses are the primary reason why they carry a credit card balance from month to month. I know Person B and their revolving credit card debt is the result of day-to-day expenses, living beyond their cash inflow. Because Person B, carries revolving credit card debt, and none of this debt is tied to an appreciating asset, we would classify this as **bad debt**. Unlike good debt, bad debt is anything that decreases your financial health or net worth. When the cost of the debt becomes greater than the total value of the "assets" acquired, your debt is bad debt. Yes, becoming an MD is an asset; and, yes, history has shown us the investment in school to become an MD has a return much larger than the cost of the debt to do so. The most common culprit of bad debt is credit cards that aren't paid off month to month, but these can also include expensive auto loans or any high-interest loan.

Person A, who has $500,000 in debt, is managing their finances accordingly. Person B is mismanaging their money, costing them more than $115,000 in interest alone. When Person A becomes a multimillionaire in twenty years, Person B will finally pay off their $25,000 credit card balance. Get comfortable with your debt, but also don't get hung up on the dollar amount. Instead, dial in on your action plan and the relationship of the debt to your overall income. Because understanding your liabilities is more crucial than the balance due.

More than 45 percent of Americans list their biggest financial fear as managing debt levels.[4] Because of this, it's not a far reach to say debt is a form of financial trauma. Maybe an unfortunate incident or past relationship pushed you into debt. That's a scarring experience, and if you went through that, I am so sorry. But if you fall into this category, or if you're one of the 45 percent, please do not feel ashamed. I want to help you move forward. Just like I learned in therapy, the best way to move past a traumatic experience is to face it head-on. Give yourself permission to take control of the present. Whether you're single or in a relationship, taking control of your debt will only benefit your financial future. Right now, we can focus on the process of reducing your bad debt to help you stop the bleeding. And the best way to start doing that is to get all of your debt out into the open.

LIST YOUR LIABILITIES

To be in a healthy position with our debt, we must understand our spending, which we addressed in the last chapter. Specifically, after we pay our variable and fixed expenses, how much cash do we have left over? Once we know that amount, we can create an action plan to use those excess dollars to pay back a certain portion of our debt balance above our current monthly payment. We're going to explore three different tactics using this approach, but just know, we can't move forward until we know our amount of monthly excess cash flow.

For instance, if you earn $7,000 a month and your combined variable and fixed monthly expenses are $6,500, your excess cash flow amount is $500. Now we have to decide how to allocate that $500 best, given our current debt structure. Keep in mind, every person's debt repayment strategy will look different, including your partner's, so leave your judgment at the door.

If you want to increase your excess cash flow, there are two solutions. The first option is to reduce your spending. As we discussed, managing variable expenses, like dinners out, entertainment, and shopping, is less challenging than managing your fixed expenses like rent, taxes, and bills. The second option is to increase your income. In my first book, *The Restart Roadmap: Rewire and Reset Your Career*, I discuss strategies for negotiating a higher salary with your employer. If negotiation is not an option, you can job hunt for a higher-paying position or take up a side gig. Whether you reduce your outflow or increase your inflow, the larger this excess amount is, the faster you can accelerate paying off your debt.

Before discussing which of the three debt repayment models is right for you, we have to lay out all of our debt. I recommend creating a spreadsheet like this so you can update your monthly debt balances:

Institution	Interest Rate (%)	My Monthly Payment ($)	Remaining Balance ($)

Here's an example of what yours might look like filled out:

Institution	Interest Rate (%)	My Monthly Payment ($)	Remaining Balance ($)
Credit card one	21	450	2,500
Credit card two	23	300	1,100
Student loan	5.5	575	55,000
Auto loan	6	510	17,000
Mortgage	6.9	2,100	250,000

Now, analyze your debt. Look for the liability with the highest interest rate. Highlight it. Do you see this line item? You *cannot* accumulate any more of this debt. Maybe this is a credit card or a personal loan. If the debt is not tied to an appreciating asset, like a home, we cannot increase this balance under any circumstance. By any means necessary—cut your cards, stop your personal loan, wear a shock collar, whatever needs to be done, *do it right now*! If you continue to rack up high-interest-rate debt, it's like continually gashing your hand wide open. Do yourself a financial favor and put the "knife" down.

GETTING YOU OUT OF DEBT

There are three models you can use to pay back debt. There is no "wrong" strategy. It really just comes down to your comfort and unique financial situation.

Model One: Snowball Model: Imagine you're building a snowman. You need the base of the snowman to be quite large. You start with a bouncy ball size of snow, shaping it in your hands to make sure it's compact, then you gradually add more snow, and as you start rolling it throughout the snow the ball is getting big, and it's getting big pretty damn fast until the ball becomes massive (see figure 4). Momentum was fierce and the snowball got significantly bigger—perfect for the base on a snowman. It may sound weird, but I want you to consider this method with your debt.

Figure 4

Refer to your list of liabilities on page 131 and follow these steps:

1. Identify your smallest debt, regardless of interest rate.
2. Make the minimum balance payments on all of your
    debts, *except* the smallest.
3. Using your excess cash dollars, pay as much as possible
    to your smallest debt.
4. Once your smallest debt is paid off, repeat this cycle
    until you're debt free.[5]

Dave Ramsey, a financial TV and radio personality, is a fierce supporter of the Snowball Model. Over the past twenty-five years, he has helped millions of people pay back their debt. There's no question that the Snowball Model is effective. But it's not my favorite strategy.

By starting with paying back the smallest amount first, you're creating a momentum shift. The same momentum shift you see when you're building that snowball, slow at first but fast and furious and staying consistent with your process. If you haven't gone to the gym in a year, and now you want to get back in the swing of things, your likelihood of success is going to be much higher if you set a small goal, like committing to going to the gym only once a week. It's going to take a while before you start noticing results, but you're building up momentum and slowly shifting your behaviors— which is great! Going to the gym once a week is a hell of a lot better than not going at all.

On the contrary, if you feel like you're bleeding all over the floor and immediately need stitches for your debt, I'm not sure this is the right approach. The best model is the equivalent of saying I'm going to the gym five days a week. You're going to accomplish in one week what would have taken you five weeks with the snowball method. So, if you're ready to take out this debt by the knees and get cold turkey with me, I recommend the Avalanche Model. If you need a slower transition, the Snowball Model is for you. It's not my favorite, but if it's for you, who cares what my favorite is. It's your money, not mine.

Model Two: Avalanche Model: Unlike a tiny snowball, an avalanche is when a huge mass of snow falls off the side of a mountain. Once it starts rolling, there's no force that can stop it. If you want to save the biggest dollar amount and pay your debt back faster, this is the model for you.

Refer to your list of liabilities and follow these steps:

1. Identify your debt with the highest interest rate, *not* balance.
2. Make the minimum balance payments on all of your debts, *except* the debt with the highest interest rate.
3. Using your excess cash flow, pay as much as possible to your highest-interest-rate debt.
4. Once your highest-interest-rate debt is paid off, repeat this cycle with your next highest-interest-rate debt until you're debt free.[6]

The highest interest rate debt will cost you the most, so let's forget about balance and snowball momentum and chop the amount of our cash going to the interest. Keep in mind, this approach is not for the faint of heart. This requires a massive behavior shift. Think back to the gym example. Working out five days a week is going to suck, but three, six, twelve months from now, the rewards will pay dividends. You are essentially attacking the dollars and cents in the fastest manner possible. You'll have to be consistent, but if you do you will save yourself so much damn money and will have your debt eliminated faster than you can imagine. The same logic can be applied to the Avalanche Model. Are you ready to kick debt to the curb quickly? If so, let's attack the living shit out of our high-interest-rate liabilities.

Model Three: Debt Consolidation: This is a beautiful structure to eradicate debt, but it's a little more technical. Debt Consolidation is when you take your various debts with higher interest rates—whether they're credit cards, personal loans, or another type of loan—and roll them all into one.[7] Use this strategy to restructure your debt so you can immediately pay off higher interest loans and restructure them to pay less interest over the repayment period, accelerating the repayment period and total.

The average credit card interest rate is 23.39 percent,[8] and the average mortgage interest rate is 6.23 percent.[9] Now both of these rates are subject to change depending on your credit report and score, but do you know why credit card interest rates are almost four times higher than mortgage interest rates?

When you buy a steak dinner or a plane ticket and then you don't pay your credit card bill, there's little recourse. Banks can't take the steak dinner out of your stomach, and they can't take back the flight you already took. It's extremely high risk for the bank to lend you money via a credit card. As a result, with that high risk comes high reward, in the form of interest rates. On the flip side, a mortgage is a relatively low-risk liability for the banks. Historically, homes are classified as appreciating assets. For example, as of January 2022, the annual average appreciation rate of homes in the United States was approximately 20.3 percent.[10] So what does that mean for you? If you don't pay your mortgage, the banks can sell your home and not only repay the loan but make money off your asset. The idea behind Debt Consolidation is to use your lower interest debt, likely a loan tied to an asset, and refinance those higher-risk, higher-interest-rate debt balances.

Depending on your credit report and score, you may not qualify for Debt Consolidation on your own. If you can't qualify for it, you can have your partner, family member, or friend be your cosigner. You can also qualify by taking a loan out on your assets. For example, borrowing against your 401(k), home equity line, or in some cases, your employer.

The main ways to apply for a Debt Consolidation loan:

1. **Personal loan**—This is a loan that features equal monthly payments. Personal loans can be secured or unsecured. If secured it simply means it has some form of collateral tied to the loan that the bank could take possession of if the loan isn't paid back. Naturally a secured loan will have a lower interest rate. Lower risk, lower interest rate.

   The interest rates are typically higher than a home equity loan because a home equity loan has a damn *home* as collateral. If your credit score is poor, you can add a cosigner with good credit to this loan to help you qualify.

2. **Home equity loan**—This loan allows you to borrow against the equity in your home.

3. **Credit card balance transfer**—If you have multiple credit cards, you should consider transferring all your debt onto a 0 percent introductory APR credit card offer. This could help you save money on interest, but only if you make it a priority to pay down the debt during the low-interest period.

4. **Borrowing against a retirement account**—Many accounts will allow you to borrow against your retirement savings. Similar to the home equity loan, be mindful that you are pledging an important asset as collateral. Additionally, if you borrow against a 401(k) and leave your employer, you could be subject to a penalty. I don't love this option, but if you are ready to practice mindful money management this will reduce your interest rate on the loan.[11]

Regardless of how you consolidate debt, be sure to explore each option in depth and understand this is a mechanism used to reduce the total amount of interest you pay, thus decreasing your borrowing costs and allowing you to speed up repayment.

If you're unable to use the three debt payback methods, there are other options. I am not endorsing these options, but I just want you to know that you almost always have options. If you're stuck between a rock and a hard place, and you have no cash flow and Debt Consolidation is not a viable option, you can do one of three things:

1. **Debt settlement**—This is what it sounds like. You settle your debt for less than what you owe. You can either do this yourself by reaching out to your creditors and explaining your situation, or you can hire a third party or attorney to settle your debt for you. You may incur fees, and this strategy may negatively affect your credit score, but it is a way of finding a middle ground. Most creditors that are writing your debt to zero dollars would rather get something than nothing. That said, they are likely not going to lend ever again to a client who pursues this option.[12]

2. **Credit counseling**—These organizations can help you manage your debts in addition to providing money management services. Likely, the counselor will enroll you in a debt management plan, which can negatively affect your credit score. There are nonprofit credit counselors out there who will provide debt management services for free. I would endorse the qualified not-for-profits; I would not endorse the for-profit credit counseling companies.[13]

3. **Bankruptcy**—This is last, last resort shit right here. Look at bankruptcy like a TV attorney who tells their client to enter a plea bargain. Essentially, you're screwed, but this will allow you to be less screwed in the long run. Bankruptcy is a legal process that allows you relief from debts you cannot pay. There are two types of bankruptcy, Chapter 7 and Chapter 13. Chapter 7 will sell off many of your assets in order to pay your creditors, whereas Chapter 13 allows you to keep your assets, but you must pay back your debts over a three-to-five-year period. Chapter 7 bankruptcy will stay on your credit report for ten years, while Chapter 13 will stay on your credit report for seven years.[14]

CONVERSATION WITH CECILIE FJELLHØY FROM *THE TINDER SWINDLER*

In 2022, Netflix released a widely successful documentary called *The Tinder Swindler*. It details Simon Hayut, a convicted fraudster, who used dating apps to meet multiple women. Once trust was established with his dates, he would manipulate his victims to take out lines of credit and loans in their name, and then he would trans-act purchases with their debt, leaving the women hundreds of thousands of dollars in debt. I had the opportunity to interview Cecilie Fjellhøy, who unfortunately was one of Simon's fraud victims. In our conversation, we learn how this debt has affected her life, years later.

Jason: Before you were a victim of the Tinder Swindler, what was your take on debt? Did you have any debt? What did that look like for you?

Cecilie: I really only had my student loan and a mortgage. The difference, though, between Norway and the US is that [the student loan is] a really great loan to have because of the low interest rate. It was a manageable debt, maybe $30,000. Then I had a mortgage on my apartment, which was an appreciating asset, and was very positive for me. I had a credit card with a low credit limit, but I always paid it off every month and understood the positives with building good credit. I was in a very comfortable position with my debt. Prior to my incident with Simon, I knew how detrimental high consumer debt loans could be.

Jason: That's a good point. I think if you were walking on the street and you asked random people, "Is extensive credit card debt bad and is rolling the balances from that debt over from month to month bad?" I think most humans would say, "Yeah, it's not good." For some reason, so many humans across the world get trapped into it, whether it's through deception or their own behaviors. In the vein of deception, what qualities do you think Simon saw that made him believe he could defraud you?

Cecilie: I feel he sometimes went after women from high-trusting countries. His victims were mostly women from western European countries where the citizens are more trusting. I didn't come from a rich family, but some of his victims did come from wealthy families, and they were able to pay off the debt right away and brush the incident under the rug. But Simon is a smart guy. He knew I had my apartment, and he knew I would likely have good credit, which meant I could obtain a credit card quite easily. Which I did! In regard to human qualities, he saw I was empathetic, kind, and helpful. I believe we all should behave this way, but then you have fraudsters that take advantage of these qualities, and I'm like, "Why are we putting things upside down here!" Simon went on a ton of dates, but he didn't ask for money from every single one of his dates, only the ones he felt he could manipulate. He knew after going on one date with a woman if he would be able to take advantage of her or not. All of his victims were kindhearted, wonderful girls, which is such a shame.

Jason: That's interesting. There are *so* many good takeaways there. We are taught in this world to be a good person and to be trustworthy, but when you do those things, you can be taken advantage of, especially from a personal finance perspective. That's just so backward. Now that we know how he chose his victims, talk to me about Simon's strategy. How did he use credit card companies to benefit him?

Cecilie: He knew how to manipulate the system in all aspects of the financial world. He knew how to write fake checks. He knew which banks had a lenient application system for credit cards.

Jason: Can you talk about the credit application process? And how did they keep extending your credit card limit?

Cecilie: It was mind-bogglingly easy! It was just an online form. I had never applied for a platinum credit card before. The form asked for my annual income, and Simon told me to just put $200,000, even though I wasn't making that much. Until my balances hit a certain limit, they didn't even verify if my income was real.

Jason: Wow, that is something really important to note. With credit card apps, you just input your annual income . . . but they aren't doing any due diligence on your true financial position, correct?

Cecilie: Yes. I thought the banks would check my financial statement. But Simon *knew* they wouldn't, which is how he was able to manipulate the system.

Jason: The fact that you were making a certain amount but still took out so much credit just shows how screwed up the system is. What was your income around this time?

Cecilie: Approximately $65,000.

Jason: How much in credit over the whole Simon bullshit did the banks allow you to take out?

Cecilie: In total, $285,000 in fifty-four days.

Jason: The system is designed to screw you over if you don't take control. When you had the total of $285,000, did any of the banks acknowledge it was fraud, did they help you, or did they hold you accountable for that amount of money?

Cecilie: Everyone has kept me accountable to a point. I went to the police. The Norwegian banks were not as silent. The banks were going to sell my apartment. In May 2018, I realized I was being defrauded. In June 2018, my mum told me I needed to sell my flat to be able to have control of some of my own assets still. At this point I was still waiting to see if the banks were going to take my complaint or not. So I got ahead of them and sold my apartment at a profit. Otherwise, the banks would have sold it off to help repay the debt. They then took me to court since we were in a disagreement on who was to be blamed for the debt, and I had to spend that profit on lawyers.

Jason: At this point, you owe the $285,000—do you think you should pay it back because it was fraud? How did you proceed?

Cecilie: During the COVID lockdown, I was going through the legal process to fight this debt in Norway, when I received a debt collectors letter from a company in the UK. I was really, really upset. I couldn't go home to my family because of the pandemic, I was dealing with the mess Simon left me, and my mental health was taking such a toll. So I filed for bankruptcy in the UK on July 28, 2020. I put all my individual loans from Norway and the UK into bankruptcy. I was on a payment plan for over a year, and now my credit is screwed for six years; that's just how bankruptcy works. Thanks to GoFundMe money raised by the documentary, I had about one-third of the debt covered. However, after four years since the initial fraud, the interest accumulated to over $100,000, and it keeps growing, which was one of the reasons I filed for bankruptcy. After I completed the bankruptcy payment plan, I was "free" from the debt here in the UK. Now, I can make whatever money I want without fear of calls from creditors. That being said, I ruffled some feathers with financial institutions in Norway. The Norwegian banks decided to not accept bankruptcy money.

Jason: So, as long as you don't live in Norway, you won't be susceptible to paying that debt back?

Cecilie: Correct. I hope so. When these things happen to you, you get really scared with high anxiety regarding your finances, so I haven't gone into details of it because I am too scared.

Jason: But because you filed for bankruptcy in the UK, will it always be on your "record"?

Cecilie: It will. After six years I can start building up credit again. For six years, I will be on a no-go list as far as credit and loans. The first transaction Simon made was on February 25, 2018. I filed for bankruptcy on July 28, 2020. My credit is in "jail" for six years from the date I filed bankruptcy, so I won't be able to start building my credit back up until July 28, 2026. The smallest amount of time, fifty-four days, completely screwed me over for eight years of my life. Try to learn from this story. You can do everything correctly your whole life and then fifty-four days of mayhem can just screw it up.

Jason: Wow, that is absolutely insane. I'm so sorry you have to deal with that! Legally, what did bankruptcy do for you? Did it free you of all debt? What were the advantages?

Cecilie: Normally, it would be completely erased. But if you have a certain amount of debt like I did, you have to do a payment plan for a couple of years. You set up a budget, and you're required to pay a certain amount of your monthly income into this private fund. Once the payment plan is over, that money is divided among your creditors. Filing for bankruptcy saved me. I don't know what I would have done if I didn't have bankruptcy as an option.

Jason: So you claim bankruptcy, you were put on a private payment plan, you paid off the plan, all those boxes are checked, so now legally no one can come after you for the money? But as a result of it, you can't live in Norway?

Cecilie: Yes and no. I can live in Norway, but I then would have to go through a second bankruptcy there. This is only because Norway did not accept the bankruptcy. Norway did not join in, and that's their own decision. They do not have to accept it, even though it was apparent I was a victim of fraud.

Jason: This is something I want to highlight to our readers: Cecilie was on a hit TV show that clearly identified her as the victim of massive fraud. Even though the whole world agrees Cecilie got completely screwed over, she is still dealing with the threats, emails, calls from creditors. If she's dealing with this, imagine what is going to happen to someone without fraud. Imagine *you* put *yourself* into credit card debt. The banks are going to come after you. They will want eyes into your personal financial statements for the rest of your life. That is a scary thought. So, switching gears, now that you are dealing with the aftermath of bankruptcy, I want to talk about impact. Can you get approved for a credit card right now?

Cecilie: No.

Jason: Mortgage?

Cecilie: No.

Jason: Can you get approved for any debt?

Cecilie: No. I can't even get approved to buy a phone on an installment plan. I'm renting an apartment now, and even just moving rentals would be difficult because they look at your credit score. I will be in this situation until 2026, when I can start rebuilding my credit again.

Jason: So do you have to live off cash and debit cards?

Cecilie: Yes. I can't use any money I don't have.

Jason: Now that you don't have any credit and you're only using cash, have you noticed that you spend less? Or would you recommend not having a credit card now that you don't have one?

Cecilie: I miss having the safety net that a credit card provides. If you use credit cards responsibly, there are a lot of great benefits with travel points and other rewards that I desperately miss.

Jason: After everything you've had to deal with for the past few years, what piece of advice would you give to someone who's just getting in the game of understanding their finances, specifically as it relates to love and money?

Cecilie: Don't take for granted having good credit. It's so important in the world. It will actually affect you and most aspects of your life. On that note of lending a partner or friend money, I recommend getting proof, seeing the numbers, and keep probing with questions until every base is covered. Trust your intuition until you get the evidence you need if lending someone money.

Jason: I love that advice. Thank you so much for sharing your story with us, Cecilie!

Jason's Takeaway: Cecilie was the victim of very obvious, very public fraud, throwing her into massive debt in the blink of an eye. There's so much evidence to support this crime, and Cecilie is *still* facing intense pushback from the banking institutions. Can you imagine the repercussions of credit card debt if you *weren't* the victim of fraud? If *you* put *yourself* in this kind of debt? Words to the wise—have a payback plan in mind before swiping your credit card, and never purchase something you can't afford. The implications of high debt as it relates to your income can affect your life for years to come, as we witnessed in Cecilie's story.

DEBT-TO-INCOME RATIO

In my banking life, I spent time in the underwriting business sector. I would take an in-depth look at individuals' and companies' financials to see if they could qualify for a loan. I was tasked with the job of analyzing the inherent risk the bank took on if the bank approved the loan. To help make this determination, we analyzed a laundry list of financial ratios that served as eye-opening indicators. One of the important ratios was the debt-to-income ratio (DTI ratio). The DTI ratio measures financial metrics you've already calculated. It combines all your monthly payments you make toward all your debts and then divides that number by the gross monthly income you earn. That ratio will provide a solid indicator of how well your gross monthly income can support your monthly debt payments. I'm all about pulling back the curtain, breaking the fourth wall, and showing you the finances behind the numbers. So here's my thought: The banks run the money, and since they have certain ratios they use to determine whether they can lend us money, why would we not try to get as close to those ratios as possible? It's a similar approach to understanding our credit report and score. We already established the importance of credit and how to improve it. Equally as important is your DTI ratio.

Calculating your DTI ratio (see figure 5) can help you determine how comfortable you are with your current debt. Specifically, it tells us how much you pay each month versus how much you earn in the form of a percentage. You can calculate your DTI ratio in three easy steps:

1. Refer to your monthly liabilities on page 131. Add up all of your monthly debt payments: credit card, mortgage, rent, student loans, auto loans, and so on.
2. Calculate your monthly gross income. Add up all of your annual gross income (remember, that means before taxes) and then divide that number by twelve (months).
3. Then divide your total monthly debt payments by your total monthly gross income.
4. The result, in the form of a percentage, is your DTI ratio.[15]

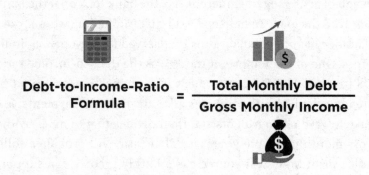

Debt-to-Income-Ratio Formula $= \dfrac{\text{Total Monthly Debt}}{\text{Gross Monthly Income}}$

Figure 5

Now that you've calculated your DTI ratio, you're probably pretty curious to see where you stack up in the eyes of the bank. If your ratio is 35 percent or less, you're in a good spot because most lenders view borrowers below this threshold in good shape. If your ratio falls between 35 percent and 50 percent, there's some opportunity to improve. In this DTI range (see figure 6), you likely will still qualify for a loan, but the bank might require you to meet additional eligibility criteria before lending to you. If your DTI ratio is above 50 percent, the likelihood of your loan being approved is going to decrease. If more than half of your monthly income is already going toward debt payments, borrowing more money is not likely the solution.[16]

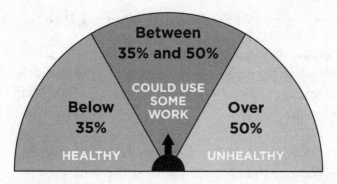

Figure 6

Based on the metrics used by financial institutions, we should shoot for a DTI ratio between 30 and 40 percent, maximum. As you progress on your financial wellness journey, you can slowly work on reducing your DTI ratio to as low as possible. If right now this seems unattainable, here are a few strategies you can implement immediately:

1. Start a payback debt plan (Snowball, Avalanche, Debt Consolidation).
2. Avoid taking on more debt.
3. Negotiate interest rates with your creditors.
4. Look for ways to increase your income.[17]

Now that you've gone through the process of listing your liabilities, learning about debt payback strategies, and calculating your DTI ratio, how do you feel? Do you have a firm understanding of your current liabilities and how you can improve your financial health to stop the bleeding? Once you feel comfortable and competent with your current situation, it's time to start the conversation with your partner.

LET'S TALK ABOUT DEBT, BABY

As I've stated throughout the entirety of this book, transparency and vulnerability are key to having a successful discussion with your significant other. Keeping that in mind, I would lay the conversation out like this:

1. Start by discussing a debt that you want to pay off. Maybe a student loan, auto loan, credit card, and so on.
2. Then show your partner the list of liabilities you created. Discuss any concerns you have about your current debts, such as those with high interest rates.
3. Share with your partner the strategy you want to use to pay back the debt you discussed in step one. For example, Snowball, Avalanche, or Debt Consolidation.
4. Share with your partner the importance of the DTI ratio. Show your loved one how easy it is to calculate this percentage and share your results.
5. Finally, ask your partner if they would like to walk through the process of sharing their liabilities with you. Suggest you both tackle your independent liabilities together and celebrate the wins of paying off those debts along the way.

It's important to keep this conversation light. As we discussed, there's a certain shame and blame associated with debt. Don't make your partner feel self-conscious about their liabilities. Rather, be supportive and approach managing these debts as a team. Think of this strategy as having a running buddy. There will be times when you don't feel like putting the miles in or when you feel too tired to continue on, but the reason you keep showing up and pushing through is because you have someone right beside you, cheering you on when you feel like throwing in the towel. You don't want to let your running buddy down. Treat your significant other in the same way. Because together, you will go further and accomplish more.

_____

My Total Monthly Debt Payments

_____   _____

| **My Monthly Gross** | **My Debt-to-Income** |
| **Income** | **Ratio** |

_____

My Partner's Total Monthly Debt Payments

_____   _____

| **My Partner's Monthly** | **My Partner's** |
| **Gross Income** | **Debt-to-Income Ratio** |

_____

Our Joint Total Monthly Debt Payments

_____   _____

| **Our Joint Monthly** | **Our Joint** |
| **Gross Income** | **Debt-to-Income Ratio** |

IT'S THE CLOSING BELL—
HERE'S WHAT WE LEARNED

- The banking institutions have a blindfold over our eyes—they don't want us to see how much we're paying them in interest. As a result, we have a deep-seated fear of our debt.

- ○ Solution: Exposure therapy. Get all your debt, interest rates, and monthly payments out in the open.
- ○ Use the liability table to organize your debt and update it monthly.
- ○ Share this information with your partner and ask them to do the same.
- Finding a debt payback strategy that works for you:
  - ○ Snowball—Pay off your smallest debt first, regardless of interest rate. Keep building momentum until you eliminate your debt completely.
  - ○ Avalanche—Attack the highest-interest-rate debt first. Once that's paid, go to the next highest interest rate, and so forth. This is the fastest way to eradicate debt.
  - ○ Debt Consolidation—Take your various debts, credit cards, home equity, student loans, and roll them all into one, lower interest rate loan. This is a way to restructure your debt so you pay less interest.
- Cecilie Fjellhøy from Netflix's *The Tinder Swindler* was scammed into $285,000 in credit card debt in fifty-four days.
  - ○ How she used bankruptcy to her advantage.
  - ○ Think twice before you swipe (your credit card and on Tinder).
- Understanding your debt-to-income ratio.
  - ○ Your monthly debt payments ÷ your monthly gross income.
  - ○ Aim for a DTI ratio between 30 and 40 percent maximum.
  - ○ Four ways to lower your DTI ratio today.

8

WHAT'S YOUR
NET WORTH?

Learning How to Protect and Acquire Assets as a Couple

Okay, boomers. Let's put down the landline and talk about Zoomers.

Generation Z, or individuals born between 1997 and 2012, are notorious for being open. Look at TikTok. Your For You Page (FYP) will promote a large array of videos ranging from hilarious hookup stories and celebrity conspiracy theories to serious topics on mental health struggles and advice for overcoming trauma.

Gen Z uses social media as their megaphone to voice their opinions on politics, equality, and health issues. Growing up with the internet at their fingertips, Zoomers have transformed from creating vines like Damn Daniel to developing legitimate information and community action platforms on Instagram, YouTube, and TikTok.

Curated images and reels of photoshopped models detailing their lavish, exotic trips, the absence of "regular" work apparent, have messed with the minds of this demographic. Gen Z is slogging away from nine to five, taking the occasional bathroom break to look at their phone just to see a video of an influencer sailing on a yacht along the Amalfi coast, Aperol Spritz in her left hand and a beautiful celebrity doppelganger on her right. And here you are, flushing the toilet with your shoe so you don't touch the handle. Experiencing that shit (pun intended) on a daily basis is going to mess with your head. Approximately three-quarters of Gen Zers said that social media makes them feel less prosperous and behind in accomplishing their life goals because they see so many others around them succeeding.[1] But here's the thing—they aren't talking about it! Especially when it comes to money.

The most vocal group out there would literally rather talk about *anything* other than financial status. Religion? Check. Politics? Check. Sex life? Check. Drunken escapades? Check. Drugs? Check. Infertility? Check. Depression? Check. Anxiety? Check. Parenting struggles? Check. Financial status? Whoa, back the hell up. Classic "taboo" topics are game for Gen Z, except for money. In fact, if the subject comes up, they will "filter their finances." Just like you see on Instagram, Zoomers will airbrush and gloss over their situation to save face, attempting to keep up with their friends and followers.[2]

This goes hand in hand with the "soft-life" mentality displayed on TikTok, where the quality and ease of life greatly outweighs the desire for extra savings. I'm all for letting your money work for you, rather than the traditional mindset of working for your money, but be cautious you don't become controlled by debt. This soft-life notion is a stark contrast from the millennial mindset centered on side-hustle culture, which presents the opposite issue of never enjoying the fruits of your labor.[3] Whatever end of the spectrum you fall on, it seems neither method works as 63 percent of millennials and Gen Zers are burned out by adulthood.

Can you hear that? It's the boomers calling. They said, "Those young kids have more information on finance and career navigation than we ever did. There's no reason for them to be burned out." While Grandpa might be right, there's *so much* conflicting advice on the internet, which paralyzes the younger generation from making any solid decisions. Here's what Gen Z has to say about their knowledge of finance:

- 66 percent say they know how to make a budget and track their income but haven't done it.
- 64 percent know it's important to invest, but they don't know how.
- 63 percent say they have financial knowledge but are unsure how to use it.
- 50 percent bought cryptocurrency even though they don't fully understand blockchain.
- Two-thirds say they're not sure they'll ever have enough money to retire.[4]

All of this is to say: it's okay. The same way Zoomers broke the taboo around other important topics, we need to break the stigma around finances. Specifically, as it relates to our relationships. How can you feel comfortable talking to your partner about money when you don't fully understand your own financial situation? Have no fear because in this chapter we're ripping down the curtain and showing you where exactly you stand as it relates to your assets and total net worth, helping break the ice around those tough money talks with your partner.

WHAT THE HELL IS NET WORTH?

Your net worth is your life financial scorecard for your entire financial well-being. Yes, we've covered credit, financial deception, our spending habits, expense-to-income ratios, our liabilities, and debt-to-income ratio, but net worth takes into account *everything*! What we *own*, what we *owe*—it's a total snapshot.

The equation for net worth is pretty straightforward. Don't worry, we'll calculate this in a few pages, but to give you an idea, net worth is your total assets minus your total liabilities.

Assets – Liabilities = Net Worth

Net worth is the ultimate money benchmark. It's our life's work! It tells us what we have at stake, what we need to protect. It's critical that we understand, monitor, grow, and protect that number. And protect our assets at all costs, especially when moving in with a partner, getting married, buying a dog, raising kids, buying a house, opening a joint investment account, all the wonderful new beginnings life throws our way. Knowing our net worth allows us to be proactive, not only for ourselves but for the other people in life that we will end up collaborating with—a significant other, family, or business partner.

One huge misconception is having a huge salary automatically equals a high net worth. In reality, the person with the seven-figure salary could have a negative net worth, due to mismanaged liabilities. On the flip side, someone with a lower salary, maybe $40,000, could have equity in a business that is valued at $2 million and have a very high net worth. It's a moving target in which you have massive control.

A great example of this is professional athletes. Every offseason we see our favorite athletes negotiate seven-, eight-, and even nine-figure contracts, full of guaranteed money and stipulations. To the average person, this seems like a "dream" way to make a living, but the reality in the numbers is harsh.

The average professional athlete, across all major sports, is in their respective league only for four or five years. That's an incredibly short window of time to be making a lifetime of income. Couple that with being in your early twenties, trying to keep up with the fast-paced rich-and-famous lifestyle and teammate spending, and it can be an ugly recipe for financial disaster. Within five years of retirement, 65 percent of NBA players, 60 percent of MLB players, and 15.7 percent of NFL players will file for bankruptcy.

Big Earnings Do Not Always Equal Wealth

Sport	Average Salary as of 2023 ($)	% of Athletes That File for Bankruptcy Within Five Years of Retirement[5]
NFL	860,000	15.7
NBA	4,300,000	65
MLB	1,200,000	60

The driving factor behind these alarming statistics is lack of monitoring, managing, and awareness. Whether you're a professional athlete or a desk jockey, neither our society nor our system educates us on financial principles. We assume the only way to be rich is to make big money, but the reality is the more we earn, the more we tend to spend. That's why understanding our net worth is so critical.

Would we really be spending so much if we knew our net worth?

Our net worth showcases every financial decision. It's essentially the net-net of what you've accumulated financially. There's no hiding behind excuses or what-if scenarios. It's the crux of our entire financial well-being, and for richer or for poorer, for better or worse, we need to get comfortable with where we stand.

WHAT'S YOUR NET WORTH?

Over time, our net worth will fluctuate. This is due to a variety of factors, some within your control (paying down debt, acquiring assets) and some out of your control (inflation, the economy). Regardless of these factors, it's crucial to keep a pulse on your net worth, ensuring it's moving in the right direction.

I recommend calculating your net worth twice a year. It will take you approximately thirty minutes each time, maybe less. So really, I'm asking you for one hour out of 365 days, or a total of 8,760 hours. That's literally 0.0114 percent of your *entire year*. I don't care how busy you are, everyone has one hour a year to spare. You already found a way to free one up in a month; doing the same in a year should be a cinch. The first time you calculate your net worth will take the longest, only because you're wrapping your arms around your total assets and total liabilities. If you made it this far in the book, you already calculated your total liabilities in chapter 7. Save yourself some grief and use the already calculated figure.

How to Value Your Current Assets

- Liquid cash: This is the current, total value of all your cash and cash equivalents. Anything you can almost immediately turn into cash will qualify. Start with your checking and savings accounts, then look further into any other cash equivalent that you have that can be turned to cash in less than a week. Think about cash equivalents as a short-term investment that is almost liquid, with low risk. If you can run to the bank, jump online, or make the call to your institution and pull this money out quickly, include it in this value.

- Investment accounts: These are your nonretirement investment accounts. Individual or joint **brokerage accounts**, **mutual funds**, **certificates of deposits (CDs)**, **stocks**, **bonds**, education funds, and so on.
- Retirement accounts: Aka, the Golden Years Goldmine. The usual suspects are **401(k)**, **403(b)**, all **IRA** plans (**traditional**, **SEP, Roth**), **pension plans**, and so on.
- Real estate: Different people in the financial space will tell you a million and one different ways to calculate the value of your real estate. Some advisers will tell you to be very conservative and value your home at the price you purchased it. I'm opposed to that model. I want you to see the fluctuation based on the economy—to see the success of appreciation and also to feel a little pain from depreciation. My philosophy is to use the current market price. But if you want be conservative, by all means use whatever method fits your fancy. To obtain the current market price:
  - Go to Zillow.com and Redfin.com.
  - Look up the current valuation of your home on each site.
  - Add the two values together, divide by two.
  - Then multiply that number by 95 percent (0.95). That way we are being conservative with the number and adding a 5 percent discount. That should give you an accurate reflection of the value of your home.
- Vehicles: Hopefully, this doesn't come as a surprise, but historically, car values depreciate in their value from their acquisition date. But from 2021 to present, we have been living in an inflationary environment, and with supply chain issues, we're seeing some car values actually appreciate. In general, five, ten, or twenty years down the road, this value will very likely go down, and it'll go down fast. You'll want to value the asset: not on the purchase

price but what you could resell the car for in the current state of the market. Go to Kelley Blue Book (https://www .kbb.com/) to gain an accurate resell approximation of your vehicle(s). Use the mean number they provide.

- Personal assets: This includes all consumable goods that have a material value. We're not including the value of our toaster, silverware, or wineglasses. Think at a minimum of five hundred dollars. Handbags, furniture, jewelry, electronics, and so on. If you have insurance on these items, a good rule of thumb is to value these items using the replacement cost provided by the insurance company. If you have an appraisal on a specific item, you can use that value as well. When it comes to handbags and furniture, those goods typically depreciate. Depending on the condition and age, I would take the purchase price of those items and discount by 25 percent to determine the current value. If you really want to be precise, you can find the current selling point of those items as of today on the secondary market.

- All assets: Anything you own that has a value of five hundred dollars or more needs to be included. Even something like credit card points: as we discussed in chapter 6, credit card points can have some serious value. If you're a strategic spender and use credit card points to your advantage, include this value into your net worth. On www.ThePointsGuy.com, www.bankrate.com, or www .nerdwallet.com, they have calculators that will convert the value of your total points into US dollars.

Asset	Value
Liquid cash	
Investment accounts	
Retirement accounts	
Real estate	
Vehicles	
Personal effects (furniture, jewelry, handbags)	
Credit card points	
Other assets	
Total Value	

How to Value Your Liabilities

Good news. We already calculated your liabilities in chapter 7. If you already completed it, just use that total figure. If not, a quick refresher: gather the summation of your debts due now, look at the total remaining balance of the loan (not the monthly payment), and write it down. Make sure you include all credit cards, student loans, personal loans, mortgages, and auto payments.

Liability	Remaining Balance
Credit card one	
Credit card two	
Student loan	
Auto loan	
Mortgage	
Personal loan	
Medical loan	
Other liabilities	
Total Value	

Assets – Liabilities = Net Worth

Now that you understand what makes up your net worth and how to accurately value your current assets and liabilities, it's time to put pen to paper and do the math.

$$\underline{\hspace{3cm}} - \underline{\hspace{3cm}} = \underline{\hspace{3cm}}$$

| Assets | Liabilities | Net Worth |

If pen to paper isn't your thing, here's the ultimate cheat sheet: just download the Empower Retirement app. You can safely add all of your accounts so that your net worth is automatically calculated to the exact transaction. They have custom line items so you can add other assets or other liabilities. This app has changed my life.

YOUR VALUE AS A HUMAN ≠ YOUR NET WORTH

Now that you have calculated your net worth, how do you feel? Remember at the beginning of the chapter when I said three-quarters of Gen Zers feel behind in accomplishing their life goals because they see so many others around them succeeding? Guess what: if you're disappointed with your current net worth, you're not alone.

Millennials and Gen Zers are facing trillions of dollars of student debt, inflation, and an uncertain economy. As a result, our net worth expectations might not be realistic.[6] If your net worth right now is negative—*that's okay*! You're equipped with the knowledge on how to pay back debt (remember the Snowball, Avalanche, and Debt Consolidation models), so now all you have to do is implement and be relentlessly consistent with your strategy. To give you some peace of mind, here is a look at the median net worth per age in the United States:

Age	Median Net Worth ($)
Less than 35	13,900
35–44	91,300
45–54	168,600
55–64	212,500
65–74	266,400
75+	254,800

Here's the bottom line: the median net worth listed here is not a required number to live comfortably. Given the current market conditions, it may not be possible for many people to achieve. Every person's and couple's financial plan and lifestyle is different, so if your money goal looks different from the picture painted here, that's totally fine!

As a society we sometimes equate our value as humans to our occupation, title, salary, material items, or net worth. This really shouldn't be the case at all. As long as you're happy, healthy, and kind to others, that's really all that matters. When you boil it down, no one is going to remember you for your net worth. You'll be remembered for your character, impact, and how you made others feel.

"Twenty years from now, the only people who will remember you worked late are your kids."   —Viral Reddit post

JASON'S TIPS FOR
BOOSTING YOUR NET WORTH

Five foolproof ways to increase your net worth now:

1. **Find ways to get more income in the door.** Increasing the inflows and decreasing the outflows will increase your liquid cash. Increasing your cash position will allow you to accelerate the paydown of your liabilities and/or increase your asset balances. Both actions will increase your net worth.

2. **Copy genius: invest in assets that have historically appreciated.** More often than not, accumulating and building wealth does not require one to reinvent the wheel. For example, according to the **Federal Housing Finance Agency (FHFA)**, home values between April 2021 and April 2022 increased by 18.8 percent. So, if you bought a house for $100,000 in April 2021, one year later, your total assets increased by $18,800 without doing a damn thing. Historical averages say house values increase at 4.7 percent per year.[7] Let's do some quick math. The median price of a home in Q1 2023 is $436,800.[8] Using the appreciation value of 4.7 percent annually, let's look at the growth of this asset over the long term.

Years of Ownership	Home Value ($)	Increase in Asset Value ($)
5	536,303	99,503
10	658,005	221,205
15	804,006	367,206
20	978,534	541,734
25	1,185,699	748,899
30	1,431,024	994,224

Now there are many factors that will impact the resale value of your home, including location, condition, updates, and the economic condition. But numbers don't lie, and numbers tell us that residential real estate is a beneficial asset to acquire and one that tends to appreciate.

3. **Allocate funds to retirement and investment accounts.** Make money on your money. You exchange your time and value to earn money; now make your money work in a similar fashion that you did to earn that paper. Don't worry—we'll cover these topics in depth in subsequent chapters.

4. **Invest time, resources, or even capital to acquire equity in a business**—whether that's a start-up or side gig that's 100 percent yours, a business idea that you jump into with a partner fifty-fifty, or if you act as an investor and provide capital in exchange for a percentage of equity with a brand you believe in. As a company's value increases, so does your equity and, subsequently, your wealth.

5. **Pay down your liabilities**, especially high-interest-rate debt. Utilize the Avalanche Model effectively. The basic philosophy here that we ought to have been taught in fifth grade is the understanding of what comes in and what goes out, minimizing what goes out and reinvesting what is left.

WHY YOU SHOULD COVER YOUR ASS(ETS)

Before jumping into *how* to protect your assets, I think it's important to understand the magnitude of *why* you need to protect your assets. I could make a laundry list of all the reasons why, but if you're anything like me, hearing someone's story is always more impactful.

I had the opportunity to sit down with Cheval, the former bridal dress designer and *Say Yes to the Dress* star. Her name has been changed in the book to protect her from litigation. She is a force to be reckoned with, helping tens of thousands of brides find their gowns for their special day. In 2011, at only twenty-five years old, Cheval was offered a huge position as the head of design with her former employer. One of the stipulations for the job was to sign an employment agreement. "It was a long-term contract that allowed my employer to trademark rights to my name and all derivatives. They wanted to use my name because it was the name of the bridal collection I was designing. At the time, it seemed reasonable that I would have to give them the right to trademark my name as a form of protection for the bridal collection." Today, Cheval can't even use her own name.

Since 2020, she has been involved in an ongoing legal battle with her former employer over the rights of her identity. Currently, she is not allowed to use her birth name in any business or commercial activity. The contract also extended to her social media accounts, even though at the inception of her contract in 2011, social media wasn't as prominent, especially in the business space, as it is today. "I had to hand over my passwords for Instagram, TikTok, and Pinterest. I grew those accounts to over one million followers. And the kicker is—they weren't even business accounts! They were my own personal social media pages that had personal messages. It was a total invasion of privacy."

Taking matters into her own hands, she has changed her name publicly to Cheval and started a new Instagram (@sheischeval and @allthatglittersonthegram). Unable to work in the bridal industry until 2027, due to the noncompete clause in the employment agreement, she has pivoted to designing shoes, where she can directly transfer her creative skill set.

In addition, Cheval also founded the nonprofit A Girl You Might Know Foundation. The organization raises awareness about the potential dangers of noncompete clauses, vague contract language, and the importance of social media legislation. A Girl You Might Know Foundation also provides affordable or pro bono legal services, negotiation training, and educational resources. This organization was created to protect women from the same trap Cheval fell into with her former employer.

Cheval signed the employment agreement contract without consulting an attorney. "I felt a lot of pressure to sign because we were up against a timetable, and as a young woman, I felt the need to prove myself." Cheval is not alone here. Many young professionals may feel intimidated and pressured by corporations to make rushed employment decisions. "They make you feel like if you take your time and do your due diligence, the company will pass you up and give the opportunity to someone else." This is complete and utter bullshit! Corporations have teams of attorneys review every contract they sign, regardless of potential delays in production. Employees should be awarded the same luxury. "When you're going after your big dream and it's coming at the cost of things you don't understand, get a lawyer, make sure you have someone supporting your interests, and put the effort in to understand and be cautious. Don't just go in with this reckless optimism that things are going to work out." This is great advice from someone who unfortunately learned about asset protection the hard way.

RED FLAGS TO LOOK FOR WHEN INKING A DEAL

▶ Don't allow time to be a function of decision-making. Do your due diligence and seek help from a professional.

▶ No deal is better than a bad deal.

▶ If the language "in perpetuity" is in the contract, *run to an attorney*. This is the legal way of saying "forever"!

A decision made in 2011 will impact the rest of Cheval's life. The dollars that she earned in working for her former employer are less than the dollars she has spent in legal fees fighting with them. This legal battle completely wiped out the entirety of her net worth! She has been through the ringer with her former employer and is sharing all the lessons she has learned. Another emotional and contractual challenge she endured is a divorce. As someone who is a huge advocate in the contract transparency space, it should come as no surprise that Cheval adamantly supports prenuptial agreements.

Cheval's Top Reasons to Get a Prenup

- Having a prenup puts everyone on a level playing field as far as showing your cards. Love shouldn't be a poker game. Rather, it's an opportunity for communication to show what you've built. And if you're having a hard time having that conversation, you have to ask yourself why.
- Marriage is a contract in itself. Signing a prenup is just a way to tailor your marriage contract specifically to you and your partner. It doesn't have to be all or nothing. You can customize the contract to protect as little or as much of your individual assets as you want. A prenup essentially allows you and your significant other to make your own laws.
- A prenup provides security. Not in the sense that you're protecting yourself from your partner but that you're laying the foundation of transparency. It helps set your relationship and marriage up for a beautiful life.
- The more you love each other, the more you should give respect to your partner's wish for a prenup.

I cannot thank Cheval enough for sharing her story. The work she's doing with A Girl You Might Know Foundation is critical for guiding the next generation of creatives to protect their business interests and assets. Additionally, I hope her experience has enlightened you on why safeguarding your assets, whether business related or personal, is critical for lifelong protection. If you would like to hear my full interview with Cheval, on the *Trading Secrets* podcast, scan the QR code. Now let's dive into considering how to implement protection for your assets, contracts, and insurance.

HOW TO PROTECT YOUR ASSETS

If the Olympics require a lifeguard at the two-hundred-meter free-style event to protect their swimmers, then you can take five minutes to learn how you can protect those assets you worked so hard to accumulate. There are two safeguards you and your partner need to consider when it comes to protecting your assets: insurance and contracts. The dream is that you'll never need them, just like a lifeguard at the Olympics, but when lightning strikes you'll be prepared.

Five Insurance Policies to Consider

1. **Umbrella insurance:** If you're currently renting, you should definitely have renter's insurance. Even though you don't own the building or unit, if a loss were to occur, like a fire, renter's insurance would cover the cost of replacing all of your belongings inside your apartment. It even covers theft. You can get this

coverage for as low as the cost of a cocktail or two per month. It's like the financial institution that did your mortgage, if you own a home, requiring you to obtain homeowner's insurance. That's a perfect example of the bank protecting their assets. Yes, your mortgage is an asset to the bank's balance sheet. You'll need homeowner's insurance and possibly even an umbrella liability insurance policy. As you likely know, homeowner's coverage not only protects your physical property and its structure but all of your personal contents inside (furniture, electronics, clothes) in case of a loss. Remember when we could supersize a McDonald's value meal? Think about your renters and homeowners insurance as the value meal and the supersize option as the umbrella policy. It's an additional liability protection that will protect you from lawsuits and sizable claims greater than the max protection at which current policy protects you. When your net worth becomes greater than the total insurance protection you have, then it's time to protect your worth with an umbrella policy. Identify your coverage and know when it's time to supersize your coverage.

2. **Professional liability insurance:** That same profession that earns you all of those dollars could cost you just as many. Whether it be a clickbait article or an episode of *Grey's Anatomy*, I am sure we have all heard of the term *malpractice*, when a professional is sued for their professional fumble. The quintessential example is a doctor getting sued for millions for misdiagnosing their patient's illness. But believe it or not, professional liability coverage extends to careers outside the health-care field. If you're a consultant, give business advice, or provide a service, you need to consider professional liability coverage. This simple coverage has

the power to protect your livelihood from a negligence claim. Some top professions that *require* professional liability include: attorneys, doctors, teachers, mental health counselors, physical and occupational therapists, insurance agents, contractors, financial brokers, accountants, and real estate agents.[9]

3. **Deeper health insurance:** You are your own biggest asset. Under no circumstances should you be uninsured. Protect yourself and your health by going to your annual doctor's appointments. If you lost your job, leverage COBRA (continuation of health coverage). If your employer doesn't provide health insurance, you can reference HealthCare.gov (https://www.dol.gov /general/topic/health-plans) to see if affordable health care is a viable solution for you. If you are self-employed or uninsured, at the very least look into catastrophic coverage plans. You may want to consider a critical illness policy, which will provide additional protection for massive medical emergencies such as a cancer diagnosis or a heart attack. Unfortunately, when it comes to medical emergencies, it's not a matter of if it will happen but when. According to FEMA, in the past year, six out of ten American households have experienced a financial emergency resulting from medical treatment.[10]

4. **Long-term disability insurance:** Don't fall victim to the "nothing will happen to me" mentality. I hope to god that nothing does happen! But, unfortunately, we are not invincible, and shit happens. LTD is a monetary benefit that pays a percentage (usually 50–60 percent) of your salary, if you have an accident or disability and are unable to work. Think about LTD like the cherry on top. If all of your finances are in really great shape, this is a nice tool to have. But it's not a foundational tool that you

must have in your tool kit, and it does come with a high price tag.

5. **Life insurance:** If you're married or have kids, you should get life insurance. If something were to go south, life insurance is like a safety blanket for your loved ones that rely on your income. But that's all it is. Don't be fooled into thinking life insurance is an investment tool. Unless you're in the top 1 percent of the top 1 percent of wealth, all you need is a term policy, not a whole life policy. Whole life insurance is incredibly expensive and will cost you about ten times more than a term policy with the same coverage limits.[11] If you have dependents, I recommend jumping on the term life insurance policy sooner rather than later. Typically, a physical is required before starting coverage, and factors like age and health can affect the cost of your premium. More likely than not, the younger you are, the better health you'll be in, resulting in a lower life insurance premium.[12]

I get it, insurance is not that interesting. Quite frankly, it can feel like more of a pain in the ass than an actual benefit sometimes. Especially when it comes time to renewals and negotiating premiums. But you know what's a bigger PITA? Needing coverage and not having it. Paying for a claim out of pocket is one surefire way to decrease your net worth. Depending on the circumstance, you might be racking up tens of thousands of dollars of debt to pay for something that could have been rectified by the insurance company with a $250 deductible. Do the work now so you won't be sorry later.

In that same vein, having contracts in place with your significant other is critical in ensuring your relationship's protection and security. As Cheval discussed, having these conversations with your partner is not a measuring contest. Rather, it's an opportunity to set the stage for what you both have at stake, to protect your individual and collective interests, and to move forward together in a unified front. You're on the same team, so act like it!

Four Contracts to Consider with Your Partner

1. **Prenuptial agreement:** We already touched on why you should consider a prenup, but let's dive a little deeper. A family attorney advised me that every state has their own prenuptial agreement. When you get married, you automatically have a bare-bones, basic prenup agreement depending on where you live. It's your decision whether you let the state laws dictate that contract for you or if you customize it to fit your own relationship. This is a great way to start the conversation with your partner. Look up your state's marital laws and review the fine print with your partner. From there you can decide if you want to adjust the prenup formally with an attorney. It's also important to note that getting a prenup doesn't have to cost you a million dollars in legal fees. For really any contract, you can use LegalZoom (legalzoom.com). This is an affordable and fast way to have a professional contract drawn up without all the red tape. That being said, if you have a relationship with an attorney, feel free to go that route as well.

2. **Postnuptial agreement:** So what if you're already married and don't have a prenup in place? If you fall into this category, have no fear, because it's never too late to cover your assets. If you and your beau already said, "I do," you might consider a postnuptial agreement. It's pretty much a prenuptial agreement, just signed and implemented after you're married, whether that's a month or years after your wedding. A postnup details the ownership of assets if you and your partner were to

divorce. But a postnup does not extend to child custody, which is dictated by state laws. A couple might consider a postnup to help protect one partner who may not be working or is seeing income dwindle because of parental duties. It also may protect new or old business interests, inheritance, or assets acquired. Just keep in mind, like every aspect of a relationship, a postnup should not be one-sided and both parties need to agree to the contract terms.[13]

3. **Cohabitation agreement:** If you live with your partner and don't intend on getting married, or you're holding off on marriage, you should consider a cohabitation agreement. The contract outlines your intertwined interests, including property, debts, inheritances, and health-care decisions. Essentially, you're codifying your financial and medical expectations to each other until the relationship ends, or one of you passes away.[14]

4. **Asset agreements:** This contract is exactly how it sounds. In the event of a divorce or breakup, the agreement details which individuals own which assets and how they would be split. If the purchase price is less than $2,500, come up with an agreement and use a basic legalzoom.com agreement to bind the agreement. If the asset is more than $2,500, engage an attorney. Whether we like it or not, talking about insurance and contracts is a necessary evil in the world of relationships. As we saw with Cheval's story, the scars of others should teach us caution. So, even if you feel hesitant about having this conversation with your partner, recognize this: investing in a contract today can affect the rest of your life . . . literally in perpetuity.

IT'S THE CLOSING BELL—
HERE'S WHAT WE LEARNED

- The influx of financial information on the internet, coupled with the "soft life" detailed on social media, has paralyzed Gen Z from making monetary headway.
- Big money does not always equal a high net worth. An in-depth look on professional athletes "go broke" rate.
- Assets – Liabilities = Net Worth.
- We discussed how to calculate your assets, liabilities, and determine the value of your business.
- We normalized negative net worth.
- We explored strategies on how to boost your net worth.
- Why you need protection: Cheval shared her contract story nightmare and gave us red flags to look for when inking your next contact. She also adamantly supports prenups and gave us reasons why you should consider signing one.
- Top five insurance policies: Homeowners and renters, professional liability, health, long-term disability, and life.
- Top four contracts you and your partner should consider: Prenup, postnup, cohabitational agreement, and asset agreement.

9

WHAT IS YOUR RISK TOLERANCE?

Understanding the Behind-the-Scenes of Investment Decisions

**DING DING DING!!!
IT'S THE CHAPTER 9 OPENING BELL**

- Invest in your future first
- Watch $100,000 turn into over $16,000,000
- Time is your best damn friend
- Top five investing misconceptions
- Understanding your risk-tolerance score
- Risk it for the biscuit—discussing your score with your partner

Back in high school, I used to work at Atlanta Bread Company. I made seven dollars an hour and spent my time working the cash register, taking orders, and putting together the best damn sandwich you've ever had. The ol' ABC Special, what a classic. It was a good first job. I learned the value of a dollar, accountability, and the importance of a solid work ethic. But here's the thing . . . it was a good *first job*.

I don't wish I was sixteen again, staring down a line twenty people deep for the Saturday lunch rush while making minimum wage.

STAGE 1: THE CONCEPT OF INVESTING

I look back over the past twenty years, and I'm proud of what I've accomplished. And that's all because I invested in my future first. With time this strategy has worked out in my favor. The more I've invested into myself, the more I have learned, the greater my network has grown, the more experiences I've had. As a result, I climbed the corporate ladder and eventually jumped into the wonderful world of entrepreneurship. What was your first job? What were you making? What do you make today? Now I know, it's asinine to work in the same job you had when you were sixteen. We're wired to grow and evolve. Every day we're investing in some facet of our lives: our relationships, our education, our children, our homes, our careers, our health, our pets—the list is endless. But still, many of us don't fully understand the concept of investing in our future. We are growing in every way except in managing all that we've accumulated; we're still the sixteen-year-old at our first job.

Now more than ever, all we hear about is investing, investing, investing. When you go on social media, there is a ton of "advanced advice" on investing in day trading, option contracts, commodities, currencies, funds, **cryptocurrency**, and **NFTs**. While those investing tactics are sexy to learn about and make you feel like a budding Leonardo DiCaprio in *The Wolf of Wall Street,* they're quite aggressive if you don't have a strong hold on the basics of investing. Let's start small; let's start with baby steps. At its core, an investment is taking money and deploying it into some type of resource with the strategy that the resource will generate a positive return and grow the initial investment. Before we get into tactics and strategy on risk tolerance, diversification, compounding, and ultimately, how to choose an investment, let's first just get comfortable with the idea of investing.

You have definitely heard the phrase "time is money." Well, it's true, time is your best friend. Let me paint you a picture to illustrate why. The sooner you make a decision to invest, the longer you invest, the greater the returns you'll likely earn. This book was released in 2024. Let's say we had $100,000 in 1974. That's a lot of money! For just a minute take a jump back in time and pretend you're living in 1974. We're going to break down three things you could have done with that money. Since we know the future, let's see what the result of your decision would have been.

Option 1: Bury the money in your backyard. If you buried your $100,000 in your parents' backyard in 1974 and dug it up fifty-plus years later, you would still have $100,000 today.

Option 2: Place the money in an inflationary investment account. Between 1974 and Spring 2023, the dollar had an average inflation rate of 3.69 percent per year. If you placed that $100,000 in a low-risk investment account that mirrored the average inflation rate of 3.69 percent per year, in Spring 2023, that $100,000 would be worth $613,311.42. One idea that I have used is placing my money into an account holding one-month Treasury bills. These are very short-term and high-quality securities that are generally seen as the most conservative investment strategy because historically they have returned slightly more than the inflation rate.

Fast fact: One-month Treasury bills since 1974 have had a 4.4 percent return. A dollar invested in one-month Treasury bills would be valued at $8.61 in 2023. Inflation since 1974 has averaged 3.69 percent per year. A dollar in 1974 is worth $7.11 in 2023. Moreover, one-month Treasury bills have proved to be a conservative investment that has outpaced inflation since 1974.[1]

Option 3: Invest the $100,000 in the S&P 500 (don't worry, we'll explain the S&P in the next chapter). If you invested your cash in the **S&P 500** in 1974 and reinvested the dividends annually, your return on investment would be 11 percent per year, equating to a total of $18,300,309.57.[2]

This concept is freaking crazy. If we do nothing with our money, we are essentially losing purchasing power every day; it's the career equivalent of me still working at Atlanta Bread Company. Whether you put your cash in an account that just keeps up with the rate of inflation, to stay with the market index, or outperform it, our money over a period of time has the potential to grow significantly. Think about it like this: In 1974, a McDonald's Big Mac was $0.65. In 2023, we're paying $5.35 for the same Big Mac.[3] This is because inflation reduces our overall purchasing power, decreasing the value of the dollar. Now imagine what inflation can do to your retirement fund twenty, thirty, forty, or fifty-plus years down the road! Big yikes, right? Well, you don't have to be helpless in the battle against inflation. You can ensure your current cash is at least growing at the rate of inflation by investing your money. That way, when future you is ready to hang it up at work, you can virtually guarantee your money is protected against inflation.[4] Invest in your future first, so you can reap the benefits later in life. Because when you boil it down, no one can afford *not* to invest.

There's no magic pill or equation that will double your money overnight. We are not becoming full-time traders, hedge-fund managers, or day-to-day investors. Our job here is to increase the amount of cash that we have for ourselves, boost our net worth, and then find investment opportunities to slowly make money on our money, growing that number over a long period of time for our future selves. It's like going to a nice restaurant and ordering a bottle of wine. You don't have to be the sommelier, but you do have to know the difference between cabernet and chardonnay. Whether it's investing or wine, you have to be an educated consumer; otherwise, you might inadvertently order a red when you want a white.

So buckle up! Get ready to be in this for the long haul. When you finish the next two chapters, you will understand the basics of investing and how to be a conscious consumer, and if you choose, you will be able to confidently engage with professionals, managers, and advisers who can provide even further assistance in building your wealth. We'll also dive into how to manage investments as a couple.

STAGE 2: TIME IS YOUR ALLY

What are some healthy behaviors or routines you do automatically? Maybe it's walking the dog before work every morning, going for a run in the evening, cooking dinner with your partner, reading the news, meditating, or reading your kid a bedtime story. These routines are unique to us and benefit our mental, physical, or emotional health in some way. They act as our cadence, a slow, steady beat subconsciously keeping pace in the back of our mind, helping ground us through life's inevitable ups and downs. In this same way, we need to build our cadence with money. Whether that's taking steps to improve our credit score, limit spending, eradicate debt, or acquire assets, we need to implement healthy, instinctual money habits that tether us through the ebbs and flows of life, reducing our behavioral spending. The sooner we set a routine with our finances, the better equipped we'll be for the future. Because as we saw with the $100,000 investing example in the previous section, time is your ally.

Predicting the future is like herding cats in a thunderstorm or cooking ramen in a coffeepot; it's possible but improbable. There are so many events in our lives that reroute us: sharp turns, steep drops, unpredictable highs, moments of depression, uncertainty, happiness, and beyond. We can't predict what's around the corner. And honestly, it can seem daunting, especially as a young person. But one of the few things we can predict in life is that at some point we want to retire. When I think of retirement, I see a prune-faced version of myself, holding a cane, rambling on about the good ol' days of cable TV, VHS, corded phones, and AOL Instant Messenger. Sounds grim, right? But it doesn't have to be that dismal. We don't have to wait until we have one foot snuggling the grave and the other on a banana peel to retire! If we plan for the future now, we can expand our time horizon and check off the retirement box sooner.

Imagine you're lounging on the beach, sun's setting, and the waves are gently lapping at your feet. You stare off into the distance at the horizon, where streaks of orange and red sky touch the water. It seems boundless, as if the earth were one, long flat line. That's how I want you to imagine investing. The sooner you start investing, the longer your time horizon will be. Every day, every month, every year that you don't start investing, it's like continuously cupping your hands over your eyes, shrinking your view of the horizon. The best way to clock out permanently from your nine-to-five is to start investing today, so you can have a full, uninhibited view of life's horizon.

Now that we know time works in our favor, I have more great news—we're living longer! In the United States, the average life expectancy for men is seventy-four years old and eighty years old for women.[5] With advances in technology and health care, we expect this number to increase over the coming decades. In the next chapter, we'll determine how much you need in the bank to comfortably retire, regardless of your age. But what's one of the best parts of our growing longevity? More time to invest. But here's some statistics you might find surprising. The Ohio State University conducted a study over a twenty-four–year span that shows men typically handle the household finances for heterosexual married couples. For couples in the 75th to 95th percentile of wealth, 65 percent of men solely handled the household finances. That number jumped to 90 percent for those in the top 1 percent of wealth.[6]

Do we not see the problem here! Historically, women live on average six years longer than men. And based on research, women aren't as involved in the day-to-day management of their household finances. This is a calamitous situation for widows. Losing your spouse is heart wrenching enough, but then having to deal with banking institutions, attorneys, and creditors to gain access to your own financial accounts while you're grieving the love of your life seems insurmountable.

This is another wake-up call that we need to be on the same page as our partners. Relationships are a fifty-fifty effort in every regard, traditional gender roles be damned. Whether you're picking out a new sofa for the living room or refinancing your mortgage, each partner needs to be aware, understand, and agree with every decision made in the relationship. Especially as it relates to money.

I'm getting fired up over here! Okay, give me one second while I step off my soapbox. Whew!

Now that we're starting to understand what investing is, it's time to learn what it *isn't*.

STAGE 3: INVESTING MISCONCEPTIONS

There are a lot of misconceptions when it comes to investing. Part of the reason is because everyone with an Instagram or TikTok seems to think they're qualified to give out financial advice, bombarding us with their latest stock tips or hot takes. I want you to throw all the knowledge you *think* you know about investing out the window. Because there is a good chance that you have heard common misconceptions that are clouding your reality.

Myth: You haven't started yet, so it's too late to begin investing. It won't be worth your time.

Truth bomb: The best time to start investing was yesterday; the second best time is today. Age is just a number, folks. It's never too late to start investing. The only time you're "too late" is choosing to not execute today and save for tomorrow. So stop what you're doing and focus on making a change now. The only unforgivable misstep is doing nothing.

Myth: Investing is a sprint, like the hundred-meter dash to a quick win.

Truth bomb: Nope, it's a marathon. Investing isn't about doubling your money in a short period of time. It's not like going to a casino and putting fifty dollars on red at the roulette table and turning it into a hundred. And if someone is promising you a get-rich-quick scheme, it's likely that you'll go broke faster. Take off the instant gratification glasses and get comfortable with long-term wins. A few dollars set away today can turn into hundreds or thousands of dollars years down the line, likely not tomorrow, or next month, but over the long run. Your future self will thank you. Prepare your nest egg now so you and your partner can enjoy retirement without pinching pennies.

Myth: I should double my risk levels to catch up for lost time.

Truth bomb: Slow down, partner! The "catch-up" game almost always leads to a rocky pitfall. If you haven't started investing yet, your plan starts today. Keep your eyes glued to your own paper because we aren't trying to outperform our partner, friend, colleague, or parents; we're simply trying to outperform the baseline of where we were yesterday.

Myth: Invest with your emotions and intuition.

Truth bomb: Almost all investment decisions should incorporate some logic, intuition, credible resources, and due diligence. We all experience highs and lows every day: happiness, sadness, fear, anger, contempt, surprise, disgust. We cannot make investing decisions based on emotional shifts. We're avoiding gambling by all means, but we can learn from gamblers. When it comes to gambling, the worst thing a gambler can do is let their recent wins or losses knock them off kilter emotionally and influence their decisions. This is called tilt. Most gamblers are influenced by emotion, or tilt, and make irrational decisions against what probability says, leaving them with a massive loss. Another great example of tilt and what not to do with investing is from professional golfer John Daly. Immediately after winning $750,000 from the World Golf Championship in San Francisco, Daly flew to Las Vegas, and lost $1.65 million in five hours, including $600,000 in the first thirty minutes! As an outsider, it's easy to say he should have stopped while he was ahead, but that's not how tilt works. It grabs your emotions, convincing your psyche that the next hand will be the one you win. The concept of tilt is one to avoid at all costs when it comes to investing. Instead of being influenced by emotion when your investment dips in value (because at some point, it will), read the news and try to understand what outside forces are influencing your accounts. The market will rise and fall like a wave. Don't freak out and pull out your investment if it starts bleeding. Instead, separate emotion from all decisions and rely on facts rather than falling victim to tilt.[7]

Myth: You hear someone talking about an opportunity and you go all in.

Truth bomb: Maybe it's a friend, colleague, someone on social media—they talk about a stock, and so you decide to over-allocate and buy in! Stop, drop, and roll! That hot tip is almost always old investment news. The best investors in the world diversify so that they can appropriately weather specific industry challenges or economic downturns. Doing this reduces the overall risk and will reduce the swings. When one market sector goes up, another market sector might go down, balancing the gain and loss out. Here's a digestible example: During the peak of COVID, if you were exposed in the technology sector (Zoom, Dell, Microsoft), you would have had material double-digit returns, maybe even triple-digit returns. If you were all in on the travel sector during that time (airlines, cruise lines, hotels), you would have lost money. Being able to diversify your investment selection to proactively prepare for market shifts mitigates those swings and helps foster your financial portfolio's growth. In short: unless you are an industry expert, don't put all your eggs in one basket. Diversification is imperative to mitigate risk.

Myth: Investing is just gambling on companies. It's too risky.

Truth bomb: With gambling, the longer you do it and the more times you do it, the more assured you are of losing money to the casinos; if that weren't the case, then why would casinos be in business and even exist in the first place? With investing, the longer you do it and the more days you invest, the more likely you are to make money. Over a short time period, gambling and investing can seem the same, but with more time, they become polar opposites: one is virtually guaranteed to lose you money, while the other has a somewhat similar probability of making you money. But I get it—everyone gets nervous about the stock market. You work hard to accumulate wealth and then you leave it up to chance? When things are taking a turn for the worse and the market goes down, it's totally normal to question if you should pull your money out. It almost feels like you're throwing cash away at a poker table. And although it's kind of common knowledge that the stock market will always pick up again, and you want to follow the adage of "buy low, sell high," take a peek at history. In the past twenty-four years, we've experienced three different recessions, including the Great Recession of 2008. Taking the tumultuous times into account, if you invested $250,000 in the S&P 500 in 2000 and rode the stock market roller coaster, you would have $1,120,188 in Spring 2023.[8] In 2009, at the lowest point in the recession, your investment would be down 51 percent, bringing the total value to $123,806. You would have lost over $125,000 at this point. Your knee-jerk reaction would be to "pull the money out, *pronto!*" But the stock market starts climbing in subsequent years and ends up more than quadrupling your original investment. The moral of the story: when your gut tells you to take the money and run, you should probably ignore it. Fortune favors the brave, not the fickle.

Have you ever believed any of these common misconceptions? It's okay if you did. I want to highlight the stark contrast between what we believe is real and what is factual. Investing is a convoluted topic that gets muddled by different opinions or personal agendas. I want to simplify the process. I'm going to peel back the onion and show you all the different layers that make up investing. We've already peeled back the importance of time; now we need to delve into risk.

STAGE 4:
WHAT'S YOUR RISK-TOLERANCE SCORE?

Identifying your risk tolerance is the single most important step when it comes to investing. When you think of "risk," what's the first word that comes to mind? Is it excitement? Danger? Opportunity? Uncertainty? Or something else? We're going to put a magnifying glass on how you view and approach risk. Because, believe it or not, risk and your tolerance for risk hugely affect your investment portfolio.

When you meet with a financial adviser, they have to understand your entire financial profile, your debt, assets, exactly what you earn, spend, what you have accumulated, your liabilities, and net worth. Pretty much everything we've discussed so far in this book. After they have a grasp on your financial baseline, the adviser will go through exercises to understand your risk tolerance as it relates to investing. This helps the adviser select the proper investment options that align with your risk tolerance and timing. Understanding risk is crucial, because unlike a regular deposit under FDIC-insured limits in a bank account, most investments are not FDIC insured. So any risk you take on is placed squarely on your shoulders.

In the following section, you'll find an easy, fun take on an investment risk-tolerance quiz. This is a risk assessment I put together to help give you a high-level understanding of your risk appetite. It's important to note that this isn't a full-fledged risk assessment and will not provide your exact risk tolerance for investing. The sole purpose of this is to give you an entertaining idea of how risk assessments work. This will help you gain comfort with understanding the why when you do go through a full in-depth risk assessment. That being said, it's a lighthearted way to create a very basic baseline to how you may approach risk. I highly encourage you to take three to five minutes and find your score. After the quiz, we'll dive into how your risk tolerance will influence the investment decisions you make. Please note, you can't make an investment selection until you know your risk-tolerance score.

INVESTMENT RISK-TOLERANCE QUIZ

Choose the response that best describes you. Keep in mind there are no "right" or "wrong" answers. Just go with your gut. When you're done, check the scoring grid to find where you fall on the risk-tolerance spectrum.

1. **Your colleague asks you to contribute $50 to the office lottery pool, as they are buying tickets for the office. How do you proceed?**
   a. Say no, gambling ain't your thing.
   b. Go in for less. Losing $25 is better than losing $50.
   c. Think through it, but do it. You're in.
   d. Buy in for $100 to increase your likelihood of winning and increase your payout if you do win.

2. **How would your friends describe you?**
   a. A cautious Karen.
   b. Nervous, but down for an adventure.
   c. A bit impulsive, willing to take a leap of faith.
   d. Thrill seeker.

3. **What kind of airport traveler are you?**
   a. Pack the day before, arrive at the airport three to four hours early—you never know how long the security line could be!
   b. Show up two to three hours early, enough time not to sweat.
   c. Show up one and a half to two hours early. Boarding starts in fifteen minutes: you have time for a quick spicy Bloody Mary.
   d. You'll never catch me arriving at the airport more than ninety minutes before my domestic flight takes off.

4. **You receive $10,000 to invest today. What would you do?**
   a. Deposit it in a low-interest savings account.
   b. Invest in a mutual fund, like an S&P 500 **index fund**.
   c. Throw it all in on an up-and-coming company or hot cryptocurrency.

5. **When I invest . . .**
   a. I do not want to lose any money I put in, even if that means small returns.
   b. I understand I may lose here and there, but I am comfortable with the swings knowing the upside.
   c. I am here to make money, on my money. Let's set it, forget it, give it a go, and see what happens.

6. **What statement best aligns with your investing views?**
   a. I am more concerned with my investment's potential declines than the potential gains.
   b. Both the potential declines and potential gains are equally important to me.
   c. I am more concerned with my investment's potential gains than the potential declines.

7. **Which investment choice would you pick given the potential best- and worst-case scenarios?**
   a. $150 gain best case; $0 gain/loss worst case.
   b. $1,000 gain best case; $250 loss worst case.
   c. $3,000 gain best case; $1,000 loss worst case.
   d. $7,000 gain best case; $3,500 loss worst case.

8. **When you hear the word *risk*, you think:**
   a. Nope, I'd rather be safe than sorry.
   b. A high potential for loss.
   c. Sometimes with high risk, there's high reward.
   d. YOLO.

9. **What is your current investment attitude?**
   a. Reserved.
   b. Moderate.
   c. Aggressive.

10. **Someone on the street hands you $100. You can take the $100 or you can guess heads or tails on a coin flip. Get it right, you walk away with $200, wrong and you walk away with $0.**
    a. Take the $100 and walk.
    b. Play heads or tails to walk away with $200 or $0.

Investment Risk-Tolerance Quiz Scoring Grid

The scoring for the risk-tolerance quiz questions is as follows:

1. a=1; b=2; c=3; d=4
2. a=1; b=2; c=3; d=4
3. a=1; b=2; c=3; d=4
4. a=1; b=2; c=3
5. a=1; b=2; c=3
6. a=1; b=2; c=3;
7. a=1; b=2; c=3; d=4
8. a=1; b=2; c=3; d=4
9. a=1; b=2; c=3
10. a=1; b=3

In general, the score that you receive on the risk-tolerance quiz can be interpreted as follows:

12 or below = Low risk tolerance (that is, conservative)
13 to 19 = Below-average risk tolerance
20 to 28 = Average/moderate risk tolerance
29 to 32 = Above average risk tolerance
33 and above = High risk tolerance (that is, aggressive)

My Risk Tolerance Score	**My Partner's Risk Tolerance Score**

Did the quiz and the results start to click? How did you score? Are you more risk averse or more willing to take risks than you thought? There's no right or wrong answer; it's just your personal preference, like preferring red wine over white, or hell, maybe you're more of a rose drinker. Whichever end of the spectrum you fall on, we'll discuss what your risk tolerance means and how it can influence suggestions for potential investment vehicles that align with your risk appetite. Once you understand what types of investments might work for you, we'll broach the subject of discussing risk tolerance with your partner, particularly if you have very different scores.

STAGE 5: DIFFERENT INVESTMENT CLASSES BASED ON RISK TOLERANCE RESULTS

I will beat this down into this book until the editors won't let me—risk appetite affects investment selection and return. One of the most important investment decisions you'll ever have to make is the risk tolerance of your portfolio. I don't *want* you to understand this concept. I *need* you to understand this concept.

History tends to repeat itself, so let's take a look at a portfolio that shows almost a hundred years of historical performance. I have selected seven different portfolio makeups, from very conservative, holding 100 percent cash, to very risky, holding 100 percent stocks. In between those, you will see portfolios that have a percentage of bonds. Implementing bonds into your portfolio will be riskier than cash but less risky than stocks. I then take historical performance of stocks and bonds performance over almost a hundred-year period—January 1, 1926, to December 31, 2022—to showcase how those portfolio selections would have performed. Before you read the next table, let's dive into some definitions that surround the table:

Cash: Meaning you are keeping your cash invested in thirty-day Treasury bills. In the last almost hundred years it's clear you will almost never lose anything, but you won't earn much. Low risk, low reward. You should expect to barely outpace inflation, thus experiencing almost no return in the "real world."

Stocks: In the table when you see stocks, I am showcasing an investment in US Large Stock Total Return USD. This refers to "US Large Stock Total Return" in US dollars. Stocks in the table refer to large companies in the United States since the data on their performance has been readily available. Using this long of a sample size of time provides us an excellent proxy for risk-and-return expectations. Returns in the table include dividends and coupons all reinvested. This is the true total return an investor would have experienced from January 1, 1926, to December 31, 2022, if they had invested in US Large Stock Total Return USD.

- Investing in Vanguard Total World Stock Index Fund ETF would be similar to investing in "stocks" in the table.

Bonds: In the table when I refer to bonds, I am referring to intermediate-term US government bonds since the data is readily accessible. This is an excellent proxy for risk-and-return expectations for a diversified high-quality bond portfolio that offers great diversification when held alongside stocks.

- Investing in Vanguard Total World Bond ETF would be similar to investing in "bonds" in the table.

Return: Refers to the percentage of return that portfolio would provide you based on almost a hundred years of performance data.

Max drawdown: Over the long run, I have seen that with the good comes the bad at times. Max drawdown showcases how much value these portfolio selections would have lost in downturns. Unfortunately, to achieve higher returns, an investor must stomach some ugly time periods, such as the bursting of the dot-com bubble in the early 2000s, the global financial crisis of 2008, and the COVID-19 pandemic of 2020. The table shows the most each portfolio lost during the worst downturns in the past hundred years. For example, a 100 percent stock-based investor would have lost more than half of their portfolio at the worst times over this sampled time period (January 1, 1926, to December 31, 2022), while a more moderate investor of 60 percent stocks would have lost slightly less than a third of their portfolio.

The takeaway: For each of these investors, if that level of portfolio loss would create undue stress to their financial situation and/or cause them to make an emotional trading decision instead of staying the course, then that portfolio is too aggressive for you as an investor. In short, I see this information and concluded for myself that investors should select the most aggressive portfolio in which they can tolerate short- and even medium-term losses without emotions being triggered, as determined in the quiz.

Risk Tolerance	Return (%)	Max Drawdown (%)
100% Cash	3.2	0.0
0% Stocks, 100% Bonds	4.7	-13.0
20% Stocks, 80% Bonds	6.0	-12.5
40% Stocks, 60% Bonds	7.2	-18.3
60% Stocks, 40% Bonds	8.3	-30.8
80% Stocks, 20% Bonds	9.2	-42.0
100% Stocks, 0% Bonds	10.1	-51.0

Now that you have taken a risk-tolerance quiz and truly understand how risk tolerance affects investment selection, return, and max drawdown, I have created a list of investment options that showcases investment decisions from lower inherent risk to higher inherent risk.

If you're still a little confused about what all this means, don't worry. In the next chapter, we'll explore all things investing in greater detail. But before we move on, I want you to take a beat and reflect on your risk-tolerance score and how it compares to your partner's score. Is there a disparity? If not, great; if there is, don't stress, but we need to address the imbalance.

ALIGNING YOUR INVESTMENT RISK
TOLERANCE WITH YOUR PARTNER'S

In many ways, opposites attract. But what does that mean for you financially? Well, just like every facet of a relationship, there has to be a compromise.

Compromise is the foundation of any relationship. You have to bend and flex for the love of your life, and they have to reciprocate—because sometimes we're the shoulder to cry on and other times, we're the ones doing the crying. Have you ever heard the phrase "relationships are a fifty-fifty effort"? Well, Brené Brown, renowned social scientist and professor at the University of Texas at Austin, believes we need to throw out that mentality and instead approach our relationships using the 80/20 rule. It might sound odd, but this methodology really struck a chord with me, and I hope it resonates with you. Brown believes your combined relationship effort, as it relates to energy, patience, and kindness, should equal 100 percent. Imagine you come back from a really stressful, crappy day at work. Feeling drained, you turn to your partner and say, "I've only got 20 percent in me right now." It's then your partner's responsibility to pull the rest of the 80 percent to get your combined relationship effort to 100 percent. And maybe the next day, the percentage roles are reversed! This is a beautiful example of how compromise creates a strong relationship.[9] I want you to take this same mindset and apply it to sharing your financial standing with your partner.

If you and your partner took the risk-tolerance quiz and fall on different ends of the spectrum, there are a few things you can do:

Recommendation One: Understand your pillow money. Have your finances ever kept you up at night? Maybe it was fear of not being able to pay your bills or not saving enough or a risky financial decision that left you with a pit in your stomach. Well, we want to avoid that feeling. If you and your partner have opposite views on risk tolerance, you need to find your pillow money. Each of you needs to answer this question: How much money do I need tucked away in a savings account so when I lay my head down at night I can rest easy knowing any additional risk taken on is okay because there is money in all but riskless investments set aside to provide enough comfort to sleep at night? When you first start investing and planning for retirement, you both need to come to a mutual decision on what amount you both need to serve as your pillow money. The rest of your investments can be placed in a mutual fund, or another type of investment, that can ride the highs and lows of the market—kind of like a roller coaster. By having your pillow money as an anchor, you can avoid feeling on tilt.

Recommendation Two: Meet with a professional. When we are feeling sick, we call our doctor. When we have a toothache, we call our dentist. When we need a haircut, we go to our barber or salon. When you need a professional for organizing your finances, I want you to use one. But I am not talking about using a financial adviser who may charge you too much for their services! I first and foremost want you to meet with a bookkeeper and a CPA. I think we rush to work with advisers when really we just need the foundational base of organization and advising. A bookkeeper and accountant can help you manage every expense, understand your cash flow, help advise with tax strategies, and more. Not to mention, they are paid a fee; they are not paid based on what investment selections you make or a percentage of your portfolio. Also, good accountants can then recommend to you the best people in town for what they think you need professionally (banker, mortgage broker, Realtor, attorney, etc.).

For most people, I don't think a financial advisor makes sense. But as your wealth continues to grow, I believe a financial adviser makes more and more sense because they have access to funds or projects you may not see as a retail consumer. Overall, the point is to start with your financial quarterback, your point person, and that should be your bookkeeper, accountant, and tax specialist!

Recommendation Three: Look at the big picture. Ask yourself and your partner these two questions:

1. How much risk are we taking on in all aspects of life?
2. How can we manage that risk?

As an entrepreneur, I take on risk every day with my sources of income. In the last few years, it's been lucrative and has gone well, but future cash inflows are always a crapshoot. Because I take on risk with my livelihood, I inherently invest with less risk tolerance than I would if I had a nine-to-five. If you have a large debt, like a mortgage, or struggle with cash inflows or job stability, these are factors you need to consider before choosing an investment strategy. Liabilities increase your risk, so choosing a high-risk investment option might not make sense in this situation. But if you take steps to minimize risk within your control, you could have the bandwidth to be more aggressive with your investment strategy.[10]

Recommendation Four: Consider separate investment accounts. If you and your partner are both working full-time and have the capability to manage your own investments—go for it! There are several ways you can go about this method. You can keep all accounts separate, or you can have a significant joint investment account, while you both manage an individual, side account to fit your risk appetite. If using this strategy, keep the lines of communication open, healthy, and honest. Be transparent about how much you're investing in your individual account and make sure your partner supports this dollar amount. Remember, investments are used as a way to fulfill your long-term financial goals. You and your partner need to agree the amount invested in your individual accounts won't hurt those goals.[11]

The worst thing that can happen with a couple who have varying risk tolerances is dishonesty or built-up resentment from lack of communication. If you have an appetite for high risk and your partner is more conservative, and you place your entire joint investment in an aggressive account, expecting big returns, but then there's a total loss . . . well, that's a breeding ground for resentment. You're not gambling with Monopoly money here. This is your future nest egg for you and your partner. You are a team; you are one. That's why before you take any action, you need to have an open conversation with your partner, and more likely than not, you'll need to compromise.

Protecting your relationship and your future together is more important than chasing the white whale of high-risk, high-reward investments. In the final chapter, we're going to get into the weeds about the nuances of investing and how to leverage those accounts to maximize your return to create the retirement of your dreams.

IT'S THE CLOSING BELL— IN THIS CHAPTER WE LEARNED

- We invest in every area of life: career, relationships, children, our homes . . . why are we not investing our money?
- Time is your ally. If you invested $100,000 in the S&P 500 in 1974, that money would have grown to $16,801,439 by Spring 2023. That's better than winning the lottery!
- Top Six Investing Misconceptions: (1) If you're over a certain age, it's too late to begin investing; (2) Investing is all about quick wins; (3) I should double down to catch up for lost time; (4) I should invest with my emotions; (5)

You hear someone talking about an opportunity and you go all in; (6) Investing is just gambling in the stock market.

- Investments are not FDIC insured. You need to find your risk tolerance score to help determine which investment vehicle to use. If you haven't already, take the quiz in this chapter to find your score.
- Navigating risk tolerance and investing with your partner. Things to consider when having this conversation: agree on your pillow money, consult a financial adviser, look at the big picture (what are your liabilities?), and consider managing separate investment accounts.

10

WHAT AGE DO YOU WANT TO RETIRE?

Building Your Dream Retirement with the Love of Your Life

DING DING DING!!!
IT'S THE CHAPTER 10 OPENING BELL

- Planning a vacation is like planning for retirement
- Compounding is key
- Find your retirement benchmark
- Build your Investing Roadmap
- How to invest, where to invest, and what to invest in
- My top ten trading secrets for investing

Imagine it's the night before your well-deserved getaway with your better half. You're thrilled to get the hell out of town, away from work, and into the warm weather with a cool drink. But as you toss and turn, your early flight inching closer, you can't shake the gnawing feeling you forgot something.

You mentally scroll through your checklist. Passport? Check. Boarding pass? Yes. Medicine? Yep. Contacts? Affirmative. Glasses in case I lose my contacts? Got it. Way too many clothes? You bet. Bathing suit? Sorted. Phone charger, AirPods, laptop? Triple yes. Favorite shampoo and conditioner? Check and check. There is so much to remember to pack! And I'm only skimming the surface here. The real headache is the prep work.

The battle begins at home. As a couple, you have to set a travel budget and agree on a location (maybe this is half the battle), and once you pick your destination, the research begins. Suddenly it's days, weeks, sometimes even months of scouring TripAdvisor, Expedia, and Google Flights in search of the all-encompassing "best deal"—the whole nine yards. You've read hundreds of reviews on hotels, resorts, guided tours, excursions, and searched every airline on the planet for the most direct flight with the best departure and arrival times at an affordable price point. At last, all the work has paid off. You're finally sitting down to book the reservations you and your significant other mutually agreed on. It appears as if the vacation planning madness end is in sight . . . think again.

Who's gonna watch the house or your kids? Are you driving to the airport, taking an Uber, or getting dropped off by a friend? Did your manager approve your paid-time-off request? Who is going to water the plants, collect the mail, and pick up the packages left on your doorstep? Do you have a pet? Who's watching the pet? Is the right amount of food set aside? Did you leave a credit card in case of an emergency? Is everything at your house and job in order so you can leave in peace without the nagging feeling you forgot something?

If you've checked off all the boxes, congrats. Take a victory lap—or a victory breath. Hell, you've earned it. There's a *ton* that goes into planning a weeklong vacation only for the trip itself to flash by in the blink of an eye. But it's worth it! Because you're in a beautiful location, with the love of your life, relaxing, reconnecting, and taking in new experiences together.

Now imagine if you and your partner ditch the whole communication thing. No one asked, "Hey, where do you want to go?"

"What's our budget looking like?" and "Are your parents watching the kids?" You never discussed the laundry list of items that go into planning a vacation. It's likely, in this case, one of you organized the whole shebang while the other person did a whole lotta nothing. They just decided to show up for the ride. In this scenario, chances are the trip won't go perfectly, and at least one of you will be dissatisfied to some extent. For this reason, most couples don't plan their vacations this way because both partners want some input—especially over what they can control.

You're probably thinking, *Jason, what's with the vacation tangent? I signed up for a class on investing.* Well, what if I told you planning a trip and preparing to invest are two sides of the same coin? Imagine all the nitty-gritty work that goes into arranging a weeklong trip . . . now . . . multiply that effort by 1,560. Stay with me here.

According to a study conducted by JPMorgan, if you're sixty-five years old today, and are a nonsmoker in excellent health, there is a 73 percent chance that either you or your partner will live to at least ninety years old.[1] With all the advances in technology and health care, it's safe to assume our longevity is only going to increase.

With that information in mind, let's keep the numbers simple and assume you live 30 years in retirement. That's the equivalent of 10,950 days, 1,560 weeks, or 360 months. Remember all the effort it took to plan a weeklong vacation? That's only a minor fraction of the work it takes to plan a 1,560-week vacation for retirement. Tough to comprehend, right? How overwhelming, how time sensitive but also how awesome. Can you imagine taking a 30-year vacation with your significant other? It sounds like a dream to me. It's going to be work, it will require thorough planning, but get excited, because it's going to be worth it!

You want to make the most out of your extended trip, right? You don't want to be the couple that doesn't communicate about your vacation. We want to avoid conversations like, "Did you make dinner reservations?" "No, I thought you did!" And the best way to avoid those awkward moments is to start planning now. Because retirement is (hopefully) inevitable. It's not something that sneaks up behind us and yells, "Boo." It's within our power to control. Will there be speed bumps along the way or circumstances that reroute us? Absolutely. There will be situations outside our power that come our way, that might throw us off the path a little bit. But putting an investment action plan in place is totally within our control and something we can enact today to ensure a beautiful and long retirement with our significant other. Because every day we don't start investing, our time horizon is shrinking, limiting our view of the beautiful sunset at the beach.

THE POWER OF PLANNING

Are you ready to take advantage of your time horizon and start planning your 1,560-week vacation? If so, great! Before we jump into the technical stuff, I want to make you aware of three basic areas of life planning that are correlated to planning your investment decisions, portfolio, and horizon.

Bucket One—Within Your Power: Remember all the research, budgeting, and organizing that went into planning your weeklong vacation? You and your partner chose the destination, hotel, flights, and excursions. Those decisions were within your power. When it comes to investing, there are similar decisions we can directly manage or even change. Think of all the hot topics we discussed earlier in this book: our income, spending, debt management, and savings. Those are items we can control and redirect at any point. I want to add starting an investment plan to that list. We have total jurisdiction over whether or not we start that journey today, tomorrow, next month, or five years from now. In the last chapter, we discussed how time is our ally. Now it's up to you whether you use time to your advantage. If you and your partner decide to start investing, it's within your right to determine what to invest in, how much to invest, and whether you seek the help of a professional. We'll get into the nuts and bolts of investing in a few pages, but I want you to be aware of the decisions within your power.

Bucket Two—Some Power: Then there are things in life that we have some power over, but we're mostly leaving it up for the universe to decide, like a delayed flight, lost luggage, or bad customer service. We can course-correct if these issues arise—like jumping on another flight, buying clothes while you wait for your bag to show up, or smiling at a disgruntled worker, wishing them a nice day, and walking away. When it comes to planning for retirement, there are similar situations that we only have some power over. The most important example here is employment. Without employment and income generation, it's difficult to find extra dollars to throw toward investing. And if you work in an industry that's volatile, the chances of being without work greatly increase. Being self-employed and running my own company (shout-out Rewired Talent Management), I'm a good example of this. When I look at the business I have coming down the pipeline, I can ballpark my earnings this year and next year, but predicting five, ten, twenty, or thirty years down the road is damn near impossible. Especially considering the ever-changing nature of the social media and entertainment industry. At this point, I have some power over my situation, but what's critical is focusing on the decisions within my power and pivoting if my circumstance changes. Do you or your partner work in an industry that is susceptible to turnover or layoffs? If so, think about areas you can control (spending, debt) to protect your income and investing dollars down the road.

Bucket Three—Outside Our Power: There are situations that are completely outside our power. No matter how much preparation and planning, the outcome is simply out of our hands. For instance, having terrible weather the entire time you're on vacation, contracting an illness that leaves you bedridden and miserable when you should be snorkeling, or a family emergency two days into the trip that forces you to turn around and go back home. We never *want* these things to happen, but we don't have a crystal ball and can't predict the future. In the investing space, there are a myriad of situations we can't control: the market, federal policy, banks shutting down, annual tax rates, the next oil crisis, hell, getting struck by lightning when I step outside to get the mail. So what can we do? My advice is to focus on bucket one, but get comfortable with bucket two and bucket three, because over the course of long-term investing these situations will likely come about. Spend your energy and effort on the areas you can affect. In the remainder of this chapter, we're going to highlight those investment target areas and make sure you're knowledgeable and prepared for the areas you can control as you plan for the longest vacation of your life.

Think of it like packing your beach bag. We'll make sure you have the essentials (beach towel, sunscreen, and a cooler of booze). If you want a professional to help navigate the rest of the way, we'll talk about what you and your partner should look for when hiring an adviser. When you boil it down, planning your 1,560-week vacation is all about managing the items within your power. If you're on board with this idea and are excited to start investing, let's make moves today. In the last chapter, we talked about how time is your ally. The longer you invest, the greater your time horizon, and the more money you'll make on your money. Now let's see that method in motion, in the form of compounding.

COMPOUNDING IS KEY

Compounding is the most important term when it comes to investing. In fact, Albert Einstein said, "Compounding is the eighth wonder of the world. He who understands it, earns it . . . he who doesn't . . . pays it." I have to agree with old Einstein here, because compounding is pretty badass. Let's jump into why.

The textbook definition of compounding is the ability of an asset to generate earnings not only on its original investment but also on the accumulated interest over time.[2] To put it in plain English: compounding is truly magic as it relates to long-term investing. The compounding gains you accumulate over five, ten, twenty, thirty, or forty years can generate substantial wealth, creating a nice nest egg for you and your partner. If done effectively, you may even create generational wealth.

Remember chapter 7 when we talked about credit card debt? Well, just like Einstein said, "He who doesn't [understand compounding] pays it"; interest generated on credit card debt that isn't paid off can compound month to month, putting you in a hole much deeper than your original debt. When it comes to compounding, you can either invest your dollars and be sitting on a mountain of cash or wind up buried in debt from compounded interest.

We've illustrated how compounding high-interest-rate debt can work against you. Now, let's take a look at how compounding can work in your favor through investing. Imagine you invested $10,000 in an account that earns an annual interest rate of 8 percent, compounded annually. The next table shows how the investment grows in five-year increments over a forty-year period:

Year	Interest Earned ($)	Projected Value ($)
0	0	10,000
5	4,693	14,693
10	11,589	21,589
15	21,722	31,722
20	36,610	46,610
25	58,485	68,485
30	90,627	100,627
35	137,853	147,853
40	207,245	217,245[3]

The initial investment of $10,000 grows to $14,693 after five years and $21,589 after ten years and continues to increase exponentially over time. By the end of the forty years, the investment has grown to $217,245 with a total interest earned of $207,245.

Take a second to let that sink in.

If you put $10,000 into a hypothetical investment that generates 8 percent returns annually and literally lost the password to the account for forty years and didn't do a thing, you would earn $207,245 in interest! How incredible is that?

When you analyze the table, you can see how the power of compounding quickly picks up speed the longer you invest your money. This is why I keep hammering home the importance of time and taking full advantage of your time horizon. Think of it like planting a tree. It seems to take forever for the initial branches to grow and leaves to sprout, but after a couple of years, the tree shoots up like a rocket. The same is true with compounding. All it takes is that first behavior to just invest. An initial investment, a little patience, and before you know it, your money has grown sky high.

I hope learning about compounding not only excites you but also motivates you to take investing seriously. Because once you start, the immediate impact on your future 1,560-week vacation with your partner is impressive. In the next section, we're going to talk about finding your retirement benchmark. It's important to note that how much you sock away toward retirement depends on many individual factors like age, household income, debt, and any existing investments. There's no cookie-cutter solution.

FIND YOUR BENCHMARK

Whether you're totally new to investing or already have some money set aside in a retirement vehicle like a 401(k), we're going to find your retirement savings benchmark. When planning for retirement, you are investing under the assumption that original contributions and the proceeds of your investing will not be used until you retire. There are different tax-advantaged accounts specifically designed to incentivize you to invest for your retirement. You can invest for the short term, like one, three, or five years, or even daily. The important thing to remember is that you are assuming the proceeds of your investing will not be used until you retire.

And when it comes time to retire, many people anticipate they'll hang it up at age sixty-five. But actually, the mean retirement age is sixty-two.

In fact, by this age, 38 percent of people found they're able to afford retiring a couple years early. Meanwhile, 19 percent of workers received an incentive from their employer to exit the workforce sooner rather than later.[4]

All this is to say, our expectations differ from reality, and chances are, you'll be able to retire sooner than you think.

Are you ready to find your benchmark?

If you have zero dollars saved toward retirement, I want you to use the following table. This guide was taken directly from JPMorgan's Guide to Retirement presentation[5] and assumes you want to maintain an equivalent lifestyle to the one you're leading today. The current household income is yours and your partner's gross income (remember, gross income is before taxes).

Step 1: Go to the intersection of your approximate age and approximate current household income.

Step 2: If you have zero saved toward retirement today, this is the percentage of annual income you may need to invest annually to retire in your early to mid-sixties.

Example: If you're thirty years old and your household income is $80,000 and you have nothing saved toward retirement, you may need to save 10 percent every year until retirement.

Annual Retirement Savings If Starting Today
(Based on Current Household Income)

	25	30	35	40	45	50
$50,000	6%	7%	10%	13%	18%	25%
$60,000	6%	8%	11%	14%	19%	28%
$70,000	7%	9%	12%	16%	23%	33%
$80,000	8%	10%	13%	17%	24%	35%
$90,000	8%	11%	14%	19%	26%	38%
$100,000	10%	13%	18%	23%	33%	47%
$150,000	12%	16%	21%	28%	39%	56%
$200,000	14%	18%	23%	31%	43%	62%

If you already have some money set aside for retirement, have no fear, I have another table for you. Again, this data is from JPMorgan's Guide to Retirement and can be used as a benchmark to determine how much you should have in your retirement account today.

Step 1: Go to the intersection of your approximate age and approximate income.

Step 2: Multiply your current income by the checkpoint number shown. This is the amount you should have saved for retirement today.

Example: If you're thirty years old and your current household income is $80,000, you would calculate your retirement benchmark like this:

$80,0000 x 1.1 = $88,000 is the amount you should currently have saved

Retirement Savings Checkpoint
(Based on Current Household Income)

	25	30	35	40	45	50
$50,000	0.1	0.5	0.9	1.4	2.0	2.6
$60,000	0.3	0.7	1.1	1.6	2.3	2.9
$70,000	0.5	1.0	1.5	2.1	2.8	3.6
$80,000	0.6	1.1	1.6	2.3	3.0	3.8
$90,000	0.8	1.3	1.9	2.5	3.3	4.2
$100,000	0.1	0.7	1.5	2.5	3.5	4.7
$150,000	0.6	1.3	2.2	3.3	4.5	5.9
$200,000	0.9	1.7	2.7	3.8	5.2	6.6

Did either of these tables resonate with you? If so, great! If not, don't sweat it. I've got a few other methods up my sleeves.

Remember how I said there's no cookie-cutter solution for how much you should have saved for retirement? Well, nothing has changed. Every method, every rule of thumb we walk through is just to give you a baseline. It doesn't tell you down to the penny how much you need to retire comfortably. It also doesn't tell the whole story of where you are today and why. Think of it like body mass index (BMI). You could be a six-foot male who works out every day and has built up a massive amount of muscle, but BMI charts will say you're obese. If you're looking to get a general idea, a quick report card, pick whichever formula aligns with your financial position and use it as a roadmap to begin your investing journey.

The Spending Multiplier Rule

In chapter 5 we calculated your annual spending and your partner's annual spending. Flip back to page 97 and find your combined spending number. Take your current combined annual spend and multiply it by twenty to twenty-five. That range is roughly how much you and your partner will need to retire to live your current lifestyle. If your combined annual spend is $36,000, this would be your spending multiplier range:

$$\$36,000 \times 20 = \$720,000$$
$$\text{and } \$36,0000 \times 25 = \$900,000$$

To retire comfortably, you and your partner will need between $720,000 and $900,000 in retirement savings. Throughout this book, we've talked about relationships. What you spend as a unit contributes to when you can retire and how much you'll need in the bank. It's just another reason why being on the same page financially as your partner is so critical.

The 4 Percent Rule

The 4 Percent Rule is a guideline for how much money you can safely withdraw out of your retirement savings each year without running out of money too soon.[6] According to this rule, you can withdraw 4 percent of your investment portfolio's value each year, adjusted for inflation, to make your savings last for thirty years. This rule assumes that your investment portfolio earns an average annual rate of return of at least 4 percent.[7] For example, if you have a $1 million portfolio, you and your partner could withdraw $40,000 (4 percent of $1 million) to live on the first year of retirement and adjust that number for inflation in subsequent years.

As you can see, everyone has a different rule of thumb when it comes to retirement savings. No method is inherently right or wrong. That said, picking the best guide for you is a decision totally within your power. And that choice is one you and your partner will have to analyze to ensure it fits your lifestyle.

Now is the perfect time to have that conversation. So dream a little. When do you want to pack your luggage and take that extended vacation with your partner?

What age I want to retire: _____

What age my partner wants to retire: _____

We still haven't delved into investing strategies (don't worry—it's coming!), but hopefully now you have a good idea where you are today versus your retirement benchmark. Maybe this information surprised you, or maybe you feel overwhelmed. I don't want you to feel discouraged based on these numbers. Be motivated and incentivized to plan for that glorious 1,560-week vacation with your loved one! You saw the power of compounding. If you start your investing journey today, time will be in your favor, making planning your extended trip more manageable.

INVESTING ROADMAP

There are three questions that constantly flood my DMs:

1. "Jason, *how* do I start investing?"
2. "Jason, *where* should I invest?"
3. "Jason, *what* should I invest in?"

It's difficult to answer these questions in an entire book let alone a fifteen-second Instagram slide. But I think I found a solution: I've put together an Investing Roadmap. This five-step guide tells you all things you should have in place *before* investing. As you navigate through this roadmap with your partner, you might find you're at different stages. That's okay. If you're on step 1 and your partner is on step 3, continue forging your own individual path down the Investing Roadmap, keeping open lines of communication when progress is made or setbacks arise. Sooner rather than later, you both will end up on the same page if you keep working through the steps in this guide and are financially transparent with each other. All right, now let's get this investing trip started!

Jason's Five Boxes to Have Checked *Before* You Invest

1. Get Out of Jail: Think of this as your "Oh, crap" money. You hope you never have to use it, but it's there just in case you-know-what hits the fan. Most financial emergencies come from unemployment, medical treatment, or car damage.[8] No one plans on these terrible things happening, but it is unfortunately the nature of the world. You might be reading this and have a medical condition, where the likelihood of a medical expense could be greater. Or you might have a job that lacks sustainability or security. For instance, the emergency reserve needed for a stable position like a teacher is drastically different from that of a 1099 freelance worker. You and your partner have to analyze how susceptible your family is to an emergency based on your own unique situation.

Based on research from JPMorgan, if your household income falls within the $50,000 to $150,000 range, you'll need anywhere from six to thirteen weeks of reserve income. If you work in a stable industry, or are more risk tolerant, you would likely fall on the lower end of this reserve range. If you want to be uber cautious, then increase your emergency fund to fall on the upper end of this scale. For couples with a household income of $150,000 or greater, you'll need seven to sixteen weeks of emergency savings. Again, adjust your reserves based on your risk tolerance.

Any funds in your get out of jail account need to be available instantly. In the finance world we call these liquid funds. If things go south, you want to have that cash in your hand as soon as possible. I suggest depositing this money in a high-yield savings account, money market account, one-month Treasury bill, or short-term certificate of deposit (CD). Whichever is yielding the best interest rate is likely the best move.

> **Pit Stop:** Based on your analysis, how much should you and your partner have saved in your get out of jail account?

How much do you have now? _____

If your current reserve balance aligns with the guide, then move on to step 2.

2. Show Me the Free Money: If your employer offers a retirement match, in the form of a defined contribution plan, you *must* take advantage of it. A defined contribution plan is when an employer and employee both contribute to an employee's retirement account, like a 401(k). Sometimes the employer will match the employee's contribution up to a set percentage.[9] The match provided by your employer is *free money*. The year I left the bank, my base salary was $165,000, and for every dollar I deployed into my 401(k), my employer would match it up to 6 percent of my salary. I took advantage of this benefit and was instantly saving 12 percent of my gross income toward retirement, at a cost to me of only 6 percent.

Let's look at the numbers: $165,000 x 0.06 = $9,900. My employer is pretty much offering me a $9,900 bonus to put toward investing. Plus the 6 percent I contributed gave me an annual retirement savings of $19,800. How awesome is that! Well, here's another pro tip: every dollar you put toward your defined contribution plan reduces your taxable income. Since my salary was $165,000 and I contributed $9,900, I'm being taxed only on $155,100 of my annual income. It's a win-win situation. Every percentage of the retirement match you take advantage of is like collecting another gold star in *Super Mario Bros*. If you collect them all, you'll unlock the next level of the Investing Roadmap, and you'll be on your way to rescuing Princess Peach or retiring early, whichever you choose.

Check to see what defined contribution plan your employer offers, and if you're not sure, shoot a message to your human resources manager. They'll likely have a packet of information detailing the contribution plan provider, match percentage, and even a financial administrator from the plan you can use as a resource. I highly recommend working with the financial administrator to customize your investment portfolio to fit your risk tolerance, age, and retirement goals. Because the administrator is managing the retirement plan for your entire company, and it's likely that's a whole large pile of money, their services are sometimes free, or severely discounted. Again, your employer is offering these free benefits, so take them up on it.

The majority of employer match defined contribution plans will be 403(b) plans, 401(k) plans, **profit sharing**, or **employee stock ownership plans (ESOP)** in the form of a traditional 401(k).

Most common are 401(k) plans, and you will likely have two options: (1) a traditional 401(k); or (2) a **Roth 401(k)**.[10] Here's the most important differentiating factor between the two: Roth uses after-tax dollars and traditional is made up of pretax dollars. You can find more info on the differences at https://districtcapital management.com/roth-vs-traditional-401k/.

Regardless of what type of plan your employer offers, or how minuscule the match seems, make the most of it, and get your free money. Make this a priority.

Pit Stop: Does your employer offer a defined contribution plan? _____

If so, are you and your partner maximizing your match?

_____

What if I told you the free money doesn't stop at defined contribution plans? That's right, there's more free money on the table in the form of a **health savings account (HSA)**. Your employer will offer an HSA only if your insurance is part of a **high-deductible health plan (HDHP)**. This means your deductible is higher than a traditional health plan, making the premium lower. With the rising cost of health care, many employers are moving to HDHP options. As of 2023, a deductible of at least $1,400 for an individual or $2,800 for a family qualifies as an HDHP.[11]

So what does this mean for you? Remember in step 1 we discussed how unexpected medical treatment is a major reason people face financial emergencies. With an HSA, you're building a second umbrella under your emergency savings plan to help further protect you from those rainy days. Furthermore, an HSA is a triple tax-advantaged account. Or, as I like to call it, Triple H, in honor of my favorite WWE wrestler growing up. Here are the three advantages:

1. Contributions made to the HSA are tax free.
2. Withdrawals for qualified health expenses are tax free. This can include anything from contacts and glasses to over-the-counter or prescription medications to appointment copays.
3. You can invest the money in your HSA and gain tax-free growth.

Note: Contribution limits in 2023 are $3,850 for individuals and $7,750 for family coverage.[12]

Finally, because your employer is saving money on insurance through the HDHP, many companies will contribute a lump sum between $500 to $1,500 to your HSA annually. So what are you waiting for—get your free money.

Pit Stop: Do you have a high-deductible health plan?

_____

If yes, are you and your partner utilizing the HSA?

_____

If you answered yes, proceed to step 3. If your employer offers this benefit and you're not taking full advantage, make room in your budget ASAP, then move on to the next step.

3. Get Rid of Bad Debt: When we calculated your debt-to-income ratio in chapter 7, did you find you have a lot of bad debt? If so, did you pick a debt paydown method (Snowball, Avalanche, or Debt Consolidation)? Well, I have good news for you. If you have high-interest-rate debt and still haven't picked a method to tackle it, now is your chance. If you already picked a method—congratulations, keep it up. Either way, you need to take care of your bad debt before continuing down the roadmap. I can't guarantee you 20 percent plus investment returns, but I can almost guarantee you're paying that percentage to credit card companies, giving them massive returns. Take care of this high-interest-rate debt before investing. Otherwise, you're doing yourself a disservice by letting that interest build up.

> **Pit Stop:** Do you and your partner have any high-interest-rate debt that you're not paying off month to month?
>
> _____

If you said yes, hold off on moving to the next step. Once you've paid off those high-interest loans, move on to step 4.

4. Increase Retirement Savings: Before you start getting cute with your personal investment tactics, you need to beef up your retirement savings. We know you're already taking the free retirement on the table; now let's make sure you're not behind. There are a couple different ways you can go about this, but I recommend doing one (or both!) of the following:

Increase the contribution to your employer-sponsored retirement plan. Be cautious you don't go over the annual maximum contribution limit. This is the path of least resistance because you already have the account set up. That said, you're handcuffed to your employer's investment vehicles, so you don't have as much freedom to customize your portfolio.

Open an individual retirement account (IRA). This is a personal retirement savings account that offers a wide range of tax benefits and investment options, giving you the ability to pick and choose how your portfolio looks, unlike an employer-sponsored plan. Some common IRAs include traditional IRA, Roth IRA, and **rollover IRA**. Some of the most reliable places to open an IRA include: Charles Schwab, Wealthfront, Fidelity Investments, Vanguard, and Betterment.[13] It's important to note that, as of 2023, the maximum IRA contribution limit is $6,500 for those under fifty and $7,500 for those over fifty.[14]

I can't tell you which of these methods is best for you. Like I've said throughout this book, there's no cookie-cutter solution, and I am here strictly to educate with options. Just know that both of these strategies are tried and true; it's just up to you to discuss which option works best for you and your partnership.

Pit Stop: Are you and your partner going to increase the contribution to your employer-sponsored plan?

_____

If not, are you going to open an IRA? _____

If you and your partner have a strategy to increase your retirement savings, move on to step 5.

5. Manage Your Good Debt: How do you feel about your good debt? These are your student loans, mortgage, personal loans, or pretty much any debt you have. At the time of writing this book in mid-2023, I'd classify this as debt with an 8 percent interest rate or lower. If you feel overwhelmed by your good debt, or are struggling to make ends meet every month, take a beat. Don't stretch yourself too thin by adding investing to your plate. The best thing you can do for yourself, and your partner, is to manage this good debt properly, rather than get swallowed up by it.

Pit Stop: Are you and your partner making your payments on time?_____

Are you exceeding your monthly payments, whenever possible?

_____

If you feel like you're drowning, review chapter 7 again and consider refinancing your good debt, or use strategies to increase your excess cash flow, so you can get ahead of those looming monthly payments. If you feel comfortable with your good debt and have checked each box, then congratulations, you're ready to start investing.

INVESTING 101

Everyone has their own two cents of where you should go to invest. Maybe somebody knows a friend who's a financial adviser, someone else could recommend the small Main Street banks, another person might suggest the huge Wall Street banks, but the reality is there's a ton of options and none are necessarily wrong. It just boils down to understanding and preference. Any decision you make will work for me, so long as you understand the ins and outs of that decision. The problem is most don't. It's like if I asked you, "Where do you go for clothing?" That's such a loaded question. Because you can go anywhere from Goodwill to Target to TJ Maxx to Nordstrom to freaking Louis Vuitton. And the type of store you choose might depend on the occasion you're shopping for—a wedding, a business meeting, the gym, or a wild festival like Stagecoach or Coachella.

It's similar to investing. There are so many resources, and whichever avenue you choose depends on your personal financial status, risk tolerance, timing, goals, and liquidity. Just like clothing store options, as you continue to build your wealth, increase your earnings, expand your knowledge, and adjust your risk tolerance, your availability to go to the higher-end store increases. From Rodeo Drive to Goodwill, there are people from all financial backgrounds shopping at these stores. Some wealthy individuals prefer thrift shops, while some individuals are chasing designer tags and throwing the purchase on their credit card, without a plan to pay off the debt. And all classes will execute investments in all areas, just like all shoppers will shop in all areas, even if they can't afford Rodeo Drive retail prices.

In the spirit of full transparency, here's a breakdown of what vehicles I use for investing. I have two brokerage accounts—one with Fidelity and one with Charles Schwab—I use robo-advisors, I trade cryptocurrency, I still have the investment selections from my former employer's 401(k), and I work with a financial planner at UBS. This is the equivalent of getting your socks, shoes, shirt, pants, and accessories from different stores. I like to see what's working and what's not, but maybe this method isn't right for you. Steve Jobs infamously wore the same New Balance shoes, jeans, and black turtleneck during his tenure at Apple. Not having to choose a different outfit every day relieved him of decision fatigue so he could focus on items he cared about. Maybe this set-it-and-forget-it method is more your investment style—and that's okay.

These decisions must be customized to your preferences. This is why it's so important to have the conversation with your partner and be honest with where you stand. In the next section we are going to show you *where*—many of the most common types of investment accounts and places you can go to invest.

WHERE YOU CAN INVEST

Brokerage Firms

I like to call these guys the middleman. Brokerage firms act as the intermediary between investors (you) and the financial market. They provide a platform that offers a wide range of services and options to help you execute your investment. Their core investment options include stocks, bonds, mutual funds, and **exchange-traded**

funds (ETFs). All of the big brokerage firms are licensed and credible. The top firms that I've worked with include Fidelity and Charles Schwab. Another large and credible one is E-Trade. You can set up an account with any of these firms online, over the phone, or at a regional office likely near you, where you can meet with them in person.

Benefits: Low fees, especially compared to a financial adviser, a massive range of investing options, tons of education tools and resources, and you can DIY or work with a professional. Brokerage firms are the equivalent of Target and Walmart. They offer everything under the sun and are financially stable.

Robo-Advisors

These platforms use AI and algorithms to manage your portfolio. You provide your inputs like age, salary, risk tolerance, and goals. Then they create an investment portfolio that will automatically run. It's like a Crock-Pot—set it and forget it. You can adjust those inputs at any time as your situation changes. It's the future of investing, and many new players are entering the robo game.

Benefits: Minimal fees, low starting capital, easy and convenient, straightforward index investing, doesn't require you to be hands on.[15] Some of the best robo-advisors are Betterment, Wealthfront, and Axos. Many of the big brokerage firms are now opening their own robo-advisor platforms, including Schwab Intelligent Portfolios, SoFi Automated Investing, and Fidelity Go.[16]

Mutual Funds, Exchange-Traded Funds (ETFs)

These are financial institutions that take money from many investors (you, me, your neighbor) and they invest that money in many different stocks, bonds, and other securities. So, when you invest in a mutual fund, you're not just buying one individual stock; rather, you own a portion of the overall portfolio, making investing in a mutual fund less risky. One of the most common, and one we've discussed, is an S&P 500 index fund. Imagine a big basket. The top five hundred companies in the United States, like Apple, Amazon, Microsoft, McDonald's, Johnson & Johnson, are put in this basket called the S&P 500. And how those five hundred companies perform as a whole is how the fund moves.[17] Every day, analysts are conducting research to see what companies should stay in the fund and what companies should be moved out due to performance. Some of the most prominent companies investing money on behalf of clients are Vanguard, T. Rowe Price, and BlackRock. Beware, though, that a mutual fund, exchange-traded fund, open-end fund, closed-end fund, interval fund, and so many other investment vehicles are simply Easter egg baskets that hold securities of any sort. You must know what's in the basket and the fees associated with it.

Benefits: Lowest amount of management fees and no need to pay adviser fees. If you work with an adviser, they likely will include mutual funds in your portfolio, while simultaneously charging their advisory fee. And so when you go directly to a mutual fund company, like Vanguard, you're cutting out the middleman and saving money on fees.

Direct Stock Purchase Plan (DSPP) and Employee Stock Purchase Plans (ESSP)

DSPP is when a company sells you their stock directly, without having to go through a broker. There are only a handful of companies that participate in DSPP. The big three are Walmart, Starbucks, and Coca-Cola.[18] Buying DSPP helps you manage unnecessary fees. An ESPP is similar. If you work for a publicly traded company, your employer might offer a stock plan that allows employees to purchase company stock, usually at a 15 percent discount. Since you're buying at a discount, your investment automatically yields at least a 15 percent rate of return.[19] Granted the stock price can fluctuate over time, but it's worth taking advantage of when you can. If you're not sure if your company offers ESPP, schedule a meeting with HR to find out.

Benefits: No broker fees, strong investor and employee relations, and prevents short selling. You can also potentially purchase stock at a discount through ESPP.

Financial Services, Advisory, or Planning Firms

It feels like there's a financial services firm on every street corner, just like Walgreens. The market is saturated with them. There are independent firms, publicly traded firms, firms that offer everything from A to Z, plus the kitchen sink, firms that specialize in insurance investment vehicles, or firms that focus on retirement planning. Every company will offer their own model, but the common thread, no matter which organization you choose, is that you will be working with a person. This means more check-ins, monthly or quarterly meetings, and annual goal reviews. This hand-to-hand service can relieve much of the financial stress couples face when managing money jointly. If you and your partner choose this route, great. Just be aware advisers charge higher fees for that individualized service. As a result, it's critical you dig into the percentage the adviser charges, and how exactly they get paid. Seeking returns is hard enough, but when the fees are too high it sometimes may be impossible. Be aware of fees. Here are three questions you can ask to determine how they get paid:

How Does Your Adviser Get Paid— Three Questions to Ask:

1. What are the full scope of services you offer?
2. Are there account minimums?
3. How do fees decrease based on our contribution amount?

After the meeting, you and your partner need to discuss the likability factor. Ensuring you both feel comfortable with your potential adviser is a critical piece of the financial planning process. If the adviser meets both of your standards, I suggest looking at Broker Check (https://brokercheck.finra.org/) as a final precaution before pulling the trigger. This government-sponsored site shows disclosures or disputes made against every adviser, as well as licenses, credentials, and years of experience.

When it comes to picking an adviser, I'm hesitant on choosing the small independent family firms. The majority of these firms are doing everything aboveboard. But the smaller you are, the less regulation and probably the larger the gap for fraud.

Have you seen the Netflix documentary *Madoff: The Monster of Wall Street*? It details the massive fraud of former financier Bernie Madoff, who stole billions of dollars from investors. Even though he worked with some of the largest investors on the planet, he owned his own firm, which allowed for lenient checks and balances, letting massive fraud slip through the cracks for decades. While Madoff is an outlier, and most financial advisers are honest, good people, one way to limit your risk of fraud is to use large, accredited firms. Some examples of these are Morgan Stanley, UBS, Merrill Lynch, and Fisher Investments. All of these firms, plus others, are regulated and audited internally and externally on a regimented basis, limiting the likelihood of fraud.

Regardless of if you go with a local adviser, or one of the big dogs, you need to understand if your adviser is a fiduciary or a broker.

Both fiduciary advisers and brokers are qualified and able to provide financial advice. The major difference between the two is the set of standards they follow. A fiduciary follows the standards set by the Securities and Exchange Commission (SEC) and is required to place their clients' interests above their own when giving advice. A broker follows the suitability standard, which prohibits them from selling products that aren't suitable for their clients, but the standard doesn't require the broker to place the clients' interests above their own.[20] To find out if your adviser is a fiduciary or a broker, ask the following three questions.

Determining Whether Your Adviser Is a Fiduciary or Broker—Three Questions to Ask:

1. Are you a fiduciary?
2. If they say yes, follow up with: Are there any instances in which you don't operate under the fiduciary standard?
3. How do you receive compensation?

When you ask your adviser these questions, you might find they're licensed as both a fiduciary and a broker. This scenario, as Miley Cyrus once said, is the best of both worlds. On certain investments, your adviser can wear their fiduciary hat, giving you peace of mind that the transaction is in your best interest. On more simple items, like purchasing stock in Amazon, your adviser can throw on their broker hat. This is a benefit because broker fees are much less than fiduciary fees, helping you cut costs.

Benefits: The largest benefit is active management. Your adviser will keep you disciplined when it comes to financial planning. As you evolve, they will restructure your portfolio to meet your new goals, help you manage life events, and seize opportunities as the markets and tax laws change.[21] Not only does having an adviser reduce investing anxiety, the regular check-in meetings help you and your partner maintain financial transparency.

These are the high-level areas of where you can go to invest. It's not an exhaustive list, but it gives you a flavor of where you can invest and what big players are in the market. You can use a mix of accounts like I do, or simply stick to one method. It's really whatever fits your and your partner's lifestyle. Just like we shop for clothes at all different stores, there's no right or wrong answer; it's simply preference. Whichever method you choose, just make sure you and your partner mutually agree on the decision, helping keep the playing field even. So now that we know how and where to invest, we're going to discuss what you can invest in, as it relates to your risk tolerance.

JASON'S RULES

1. Know their fees.
2. Make sure they are a fiduciary or are bound to fiduciary standards.
3. Know you don't need an adviser.
4. If you want one make sure they are providing services and investment option access that aren't available to just everyone.
5. LOVE and TRUST who you decide to work with.

WHAT TO INVEST IN

In any given grocery store, Kroger, Wegmans, Publix, Trader Joe's, you name it, there are more than 39,500 items.[22] Of course there are your staples like milk, bread, and eggs, but there's also a ton of other stuff. Whatever ends up on your grocery list depends on your needs. If you're planning on eating at home for every meal, your list will be much longer compared to someone who's eating out five nights a week. What kind of shopper you are also influences your list: bargain shopper, organic shopper, impulse shopper, local shopper.

This same idea translates to investing. When you look at investing opportunities, tons of options line the shelves. There are stocks, bonds, mutual funds, ETFs, cryptocurrency, and so on. What you invest in depends on your goals and your risk tolerance. Are you making an intense new recipe for a fifteen-person dinner party, or are you dishing up a tried-and-true recipe for your immediate family? Depending on the circumstance, your grocery list will look much different. We need to approach investing the same way.

First, refer back to your risk tolerance score we determined in the last chapter. Do you have a low, medium, or high risk tolerance? Based on the next table, you can get an idea of what type of investments align with specific risk levels.

Risk Score	Risk Tolerance	Investment Aligned with Risk Level
12 or Below	Low	Cash and cash equivalents, savings account, money market account, CDs
13 to 19	Below average	Treasury notes, government bonds
20 to 28	Average–moderate	Corporate bonds, high income bonds, and "conservative" or "moderate" allocation funds
29 to 32	Above average	Real estate and "moderate growth" or "aggressive growth" allocation funds
33 and above	High	Large cap stocks, futures, options, collectibles, cryptocurrency

While there's no "wrong" risk tolerance, I encourage you to exercise caution if you fall in the high-risk zone. Just always keep in mind while the high-risk zone might have the largest return, you also have a greater likelihood of losing your entire investment. Plus, unlike the set-it-and-forget-it mentality of CDs, bonds, or mutual funds—which gradually make money on your money, albeit at a slower rate—investing in futures, options, and crypto requires daily monitoring to increase the likelihood of success

Once your risk tolerance is determined, it's time to analyze your investing goals. Are you investing for the long term, like retirement or your future child's education? Or are you investing for a short-term purchase, like a house or vehicle? In general, the longer your investing goal, the more risk you will be able to handle. This is because your time horizon is greater, allowing your money to withstand the inevitable ebbs and flows of the market. If your investing goal is short term, let's say two years or less, it may make more sense to use a risk-averse strategy, to avoid the likelihood of losing your principal investment.

Figure 7 shows investing options, building from low risk to high risk. The low-risk options have a very predictable rate of return, reducing the probability of loss. Additionally, these investments can be liquidated rather quickly, giving you greater access to cash flow in case of emergency. The middle-risk options are the most common investments. These vehicles work best if you invest your money over a period greater than five years. Keep in mind the power of compounding. Finally, the high-risk options carry the most inherent volatility. You saw those downturns in the high-risk portfolio in chapter 9. You can either earn massive returns or lose your original investment. So, if you choose a high-risk investment, do your research, and be mindful of the money you deploy into the investment.

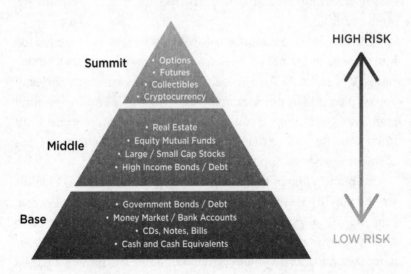

Figure 7

Whether you use a brokerage firm, robo-advisor, or financial adviser, it's important to avoid betting it all on a single horse. You don't wanna paint the entire canvas with one color. Spreading your money across multiple investments helps minimize the risk of loss. In the financial world, we call this diversification. Every person's investment portfolio should be diversified, but how their portfolio is diversified depends on their risk tolerance and goals (I know, I sound like a broken record). We're going to review examples of a conservative, moderate, and growth-focused portfolio and how diversification plays a role in each.

INVESTMENT PORTFOLIO

Think of your investment portfolio as a grocery cart. You're walking down the aisles of your local market and throw in a variety of things: apples, spinach, coffee, chicken, peanut butter, and Oreos. What you purchase is dependent on your needs and will look entirely different from the person behind you in line, who only has a pack of hot dogs and buns. Does that make you right and the other customer wrong? Of course not. The same is true for your investment portfolio.

When it comes to building a portfolio, we're not going to get too into the weeds. I'm not going to teach you how to analyze the quick ratios, P/E ratio, PEG, or ROA: that would take a whole series of books, plus classroom sessions with professors and hedge-fund managers. Quick note, if you are already there, definitely check out finviz.com. But rather than that, we're going to review what types of investments make up traditional portfolios.

One of the companies I use and highly recommended is Fidelity. On the Fidelity Institutional site (https://institutional.fidelity.com /app/item/RD_9883271/model-portfolios.html), which is used to educate even their own advisers, I found their recommended investment portfolio mix for conservative, moderate, and growth-focused investors. In their model, Fidelity uses four different types of investments (see figure 8). Think of these as the items in your grocery cart:

- Domestic equities—These are stocks of companies located in the United States and are traded on a variety of stock exchanges, primarily in US dollars. For the purposes of this portfolio makeup, these investments are considered moderate risk.
- International equities—These are stocks of companies located internationally and are traded on a variety of stock exchanges, with different currencies. For the purposes of this portfolio makeup, these investments are considered high risk.
- Bonds—Bonds are sold by large corporations or the government as a way to raise money, almost like an IOU. The investor buys the bond and in return receives interest. These are considered low-risk investments.[23]
- Short-Term—These assets can be converted to cash relatively quickly based on duration selected. Examples include Treasury bills, money market funds, short-term mutual funds, or certificates of deposit. These investments are highly liquid and are considered low risk.

Model Allocation Mix

Domestic Equities   International Equities   Bonds   Short-Term

Figure 8

Conservative portfolio: Your portfolio might look like figure 9 if you're cautious with your money and are trying to limit your risk. This example is diversified in the sense that there are investments in all four categories; however, 90 percent of the portfolio is made up of low-risk investments and 10 percent in high-risk. If you had $1,000 to invest, the breakdown would look like this: $560 in bonds, $340 in short-term, $70 in domestic equities, and $30 in international equities.

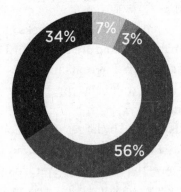

10% | 90%

Figure 9

Moderate: Your portfolio might look like figure 10 if you're willing to have some skin in the game, without taking on too much risk. In my opinion, this portfolio is a healthy mix of diversification and has the potential for a decent rate of return with 50 percent of investments in low-risk options and 50 percent in high-risk. If you had $1,000 to invest, the breakdown would look like this: $400 in bonds, $350 in domestic equities, $150 in international equities, and $100 in short-term.

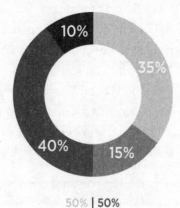

Figure 10

Growth focused: Your portfolio might look like figure 11 if you believe in the "high-risk, high-reward" mentality. Unlike our other models, this portfolio has very little diversification, placing 100 percent of investments in the high-risk bucket. The person using this model likely has another investment portfolio that is more conservative to help manage risk. If you had $1,000 to invest, the breakdown would look like this: $700 in domestic equities and $300 in international equities.

Figure 11

If none of these portfolio makeups work for you, you can look at one of my portfolios. It's a basic, low-fee portfolio I built and put $100,000 into. See the next table repeated from chapter 9. I selected a risk tolerance of 60 percent stock, 40 percent bond. A $60,000 investment in "VT" (Vanguard Total World Stock ETF) and $40,000 investment in "BNDW" (Vanguard Total World Bond ETF). Each year, I will rebalance my allocation between the two funds as markets rise and fall to ensure I stay within my risk tolerance.

Risk Tolerance	Return (%)	Max Drawdown (%)
100% Cash	3.2	0.0
0% Stocks, 100% Bonds	4.7	–13.0
20% Stocks, 80% Bonds	6.0	–12.5
40% Stocks, 60% Bonds	7.2	–18.3
60% Stocks, 40% Bonds	8.3	–30.8
80% Stocks, 20% Bonds	9.2	–42.0
100% Stocks, 0% Bonds	10.1	–51.0

Now you see why it's so hard to answer "Jason, where should I invest my money?" These models should be used as an educational guide. They aren't the end-all and be-all by *any* means. When you compose your investment portfolio, you might find you fall somewhere in between these models—and that's okay. The purpose of showing you these models is to highlight why our risk tolerance and goals affect how, where, and what we invest in. I told you I'd repeat this shit until the editors took it out! Because at the end of the day, comparing what's in your grocery cart to what's in your neighbor's is kind of pointless. The only thing that matters is getting on the same page as your partner so you have the right groceries for your nutritional standards and for the occasions that matter. It's the same with investing, so now you can start your investing journey together.

JASON'S TOP TEN INVESTING TRADING SECRETS

1. Make more and spend less. Notice how I didn't say "or."
2. If you want to become an investing expert, put the time in and educate yourself. If that's too overwhelming, rely on billion-dollar-plus tools, resources, financial advisers, brokerage firms, or robo-advisors. Don't rely on your friends or hearsay.
3. It's impossible to time the market perfectly. No one has a crystal ball and can predict the future. Don't let timing lead to analysis paralysis. *Stop* overthinking and *do* something. Something is always better than nothing!
4. Debt can kill you or make you. Use debt to invest in assets that appreciate at a greater rate than the cost of debt. Don't use debt to acquire intangible or depreciating assets. Understand the difference between good debt and bad debt, then manage each accordingly.
5. We all have exes, romantic partners that we thought were the endgame but ended up not working out. We all will have investments that lose. Just like our exes, use your investment losses as an ability to learn and grow. Don't let those losses spiral and break you. This creates a situation in which you win or you learn.
6. When you manage risk and diversification properly, the investment "anxiety" evaporates.
7. Negotiate everything in life: your pay, your bills, rates, fees, and everything in between. If you save $1,000, that could be close to $1,500 of pretax earnings you just added to your income line. If you do this several times a month, every month, you do the math of what it will do for your wealth in a lifetime.

8. The best time to invest was yesterday, and if you didn't invest yesterday, the second best time to invest is today. Time is an asset; use your assets wisely! The worst thing you can do is wait for tomorrow.

9. Time is finite; take advantage of time and let it work for you, not against you.

10. Attempting to beat the market is a nearly impossible task. So why try if you're not a pro? Find index funds with low fees that track the US market and you'll be aligned with the entirety of the market. Here are some of my favorite:

    ○ VOO—Vanguard's Index fund that mirrors the S&P 500. This fund represents the five hundred largest companies in the United States.

    ○ VTWO—Vanguard's ETF that mirrors the Russell 2000, a group of two thousand of the smallest publicly traded companies in the United States.

    ○ VTI—Want a larger net? This Vanguard index covers almost every single publicly traded stock in the United States. It includes small, medium, and large companies in all sectors.[24]

IT'S THE CLOSING BELL—
IN THIS CHAPTER WE LEARNED

- When it comes to planning for retirement, focus on the items within your power, like income, spending, debt management, and savings. Wasting your energy on things outside your power, like the next recession, war, or economic boom, is fruitless.

- Compounding is the most important facet of investing. It's the ability of an asset to generate earnings not only on its original investment but also on the accumulated interest over time. Simply put—the sooner you invest, the longer your investment can gain compounded interest, making you more money. So start today, not tomorrow.

- Before you decide at what age you can retire, you need to find your retirement savings benchmark. You can find your benchmark by using either the Spending Multiplier Rule or the 4 Percent Rule. Check out pages 209 and 210 to see the exact formulas.

- Before you start investing, you need to build your Investing Roadmap by following these five steps: (1) Establish your emergency fund; (2) Take full advantage of all your employer-defined contribution plans (retirement match, HSA); (3) Get rid of your bad debt; (4) Increase your retirement savings; and (5) Make sure your good debt is under control.

- Where to invest: Brokerage firms, robo-advisors, investment management companies, direct stock purchase plans (DSPP), financial advisory or planning firms. Pro tip: if using a financial adviser, make sure you determine if they are a fiduciary or broker and how the adviser gets paid.

- What you invest in will be determined by your risk tolerance score (refer back to the quiz in chapter 9). Low-risk investments: CDs, money market accounts, bonds. Moderate-risk investments: high income bonds, large/small cap stocks, real estate. High-risk investments: cryptocurrency, futures, collectibles. But no matter where you fall on the risk spectrum, your investment portfolio will likely be a healthy mix of low-risk, moderate-risk, and some high-risk options.

Welp, even if you learned nothing, feel good knowing you're on the right side of more than 50 percent of adults, because more than 50 percent of adults have not read a book from start to finish in the last year.[1] You made it! First off, I want to thank you, reader, for getting to the end of this journey. Learning about and Talking Money aren't always the most exciting subjects, and with a smorgasbord of content out there, you could have picked up any book on personal finance. Yet, you picked this one. And for that, I am eternally grateful.

My sincere hope is that you've pocketed at least two pieces of information: money management wisdom you didn't have before and the confidence to start the conversation regarding money with yourself and with your partner. When we show our cards to each other—aces, jokers, and everything in between—we open the doors of vulnerability, creating a stronger, more honest, fortified bond. I'd be willing to bet my last nickel you've now got what it takes to achieve that bond and strength with your loved ones and in your own partnership. You know the eight questions to ask, you know what the numbers mean and how to improve them, and you know how to start the conversation without weaponizing vulnerability. You're ready to soar. I believe in you. But more importantly, I hope you believe in yourself to live a life that is healthy, wealthy, and happy with all the time in the world to enjoy.

So here we are. The crescendo of our journey. As we approach the ultimate cliff-hanger, it's time to put your well-earned wisdom into action. Saddle up, meet your partner's gaze, and with all the confidence, love, and respect in your heart, go ahead, ask them the million-dollar question:

"Do you want to Talk Money to me?"

401(k)—This is a retirement savings account offered by employers (your boss) to employees (you). It allows employees to invest a percentage of their pretax income for retirement. The money you contribute will be taken directly out of your paycheck before taxes are deducted, which will lower your taxable income for the year. If you make $45,000 a year and contribute $5,000 to your 401(k), you will only be taxed on $40,000.

403(b)—This is really similar to a 401(k), but this account is specifically designed for certain tax-exempt organizations like schools, hospitals, and other nonprofits.

assets—Pretty much anything you own or have equity in that can be of some economic value or liquidated for a value. This can include checking, savings, retirement, and investment accounts or physical property like real estate, a house, vehicle, jewelry, or furniture.

bad debt—Any type of loan or debt that decreases your net worth. The most common culprits are credit cards that aren't paid off month to month. Some other examples include expensive auto loans or a high-interest (double-digit) personal loan.

balance sheet—A super-duper important financial tool that companies use to track their assets, liabilities, and shareholder equity. Balance sheets are usually updated monthly. They help a company to see if it's in a healthy position to cover its operational and managerial obligations.

bond—Not to be confused with 007. Think of a bond as an IOU from a company or the government, called the bond issuer. Bonds are typically used when the issuer needs to raise capital for funding projects. When you buy a bond, you are essentially lending your money over a set period of time. When the bond matures, or when the set lending period ends, the issuer promises to pay you back your original investment; plus you get regular interest payments throughout the bond's term. This is considered a low-risk investment option.

brokerage account—Think of a brokerage account as a web browser. Whether you use Google Chrome, Internet Explorer, or Safari, each browser essentially does the same thing—connects you to the internet. A brokerage account is essentially a platform that allows you to buy or sell investments, like stocks, bonds, mutual funds, and ETFs. Just like a web browser, there are many brokerage firms that allow you to set up an account to start investing. Examples: Fidelity Investments, Charles Schwab, or E-Trade.

cash inflow—This is your income. Any money you have coming in from your salary or side hustles.

cash outflow—The money you spend on variable and fixed expenses.

certificates of deposit (CDs)—This is a low-risk investment. It's a financial product offered by banks that allows consumers to deposit money for a specified period of time, usually a few months to a couple years, depending on the offering. In exchange for opening up the CD for the agreed-upon term, the bank will offer you a fixed interest rate, which is usually significantly higher than the small percentage you would earn on a regular savings account. Two things to be aware of: (1) There's usually a minimum dollar amount required to open a CD and (2) Unlike a regular savings account, you typically can't withdraw money from the CD during the course of the term. Otherwise, you may face a withdrawal penalty.

Consumer Financial Protection Bureau (CFPB)—They are a really important US government agency that protects consumers (you and me) from unfair financial practices. These guys will go after any company breaking the law. They even go as far as providing tools and resources for citizens to help them make smart financial decisions!

credit utilization rate—This is the amount of credit you're using divided by the total credit limit available to you. For example, if your credit card limit is $5,000, and every month you only use $1,000 of the credit available to you (because you're a smart cookie and pay off your balance religiously), your credit utilization rate would be calculated by $1,000/$5,000 = 20 percent. Banks look at this percentage to see how well you're managing your debt. Try to keep your credit utilization rate at 30 percent or less. Any higher than that, and it may affect your credit score.

cryptocurrency—Bitcoin, Dogecoin, Ethereum, Tether, the list goes on and on. So what the hell is it? Well, without getting too nitty-gritty, it's a digital currency, not tied to a traditional bank, that is secured using advanced encryption techniques so the digital coin cannot be counterfeited. Crypto is pretty much digital money that can be used to buy things or make investments, but it only exists digitally.

dividend—When a company makes a profit, they have two options: they can reinvest all of that money back into the business *or* they can take a portion of the profits and distribute it back to shareholders and investors. When a company chooses to distribute some of the profits, this is called a dividend.

employee stock ownership plan (ESOP)—If you work for a publicly traded company, your employer might offer you an ownership stake in the form of company stock. ESOPs benefit both the employer and the employee. When the company is profitable, the stock value increases, putting more money in the company's and employees' pockets. Talk about a win-win! If you leave the organization, you can typically sell your shares back to the ESOP or the company at fair market value. This allows you to take the cash benefits with you.

equity—Essentially, equity is what you own. If you liquidated a particular asset and paid off all the debt, what would you have left? This applies not only in the business world with ownership stake in a company but also to any asset you might have a loan on, like a home or vehicle. For example, if you sold your car for $30,000 but still had $10,000 left on your outstanding car loan, your equity would be the difference, or $20,000.

exchange-traded funds (ETFs)—These are investment funds that can be bought and sold on the stock exchange (NASDAQ, NYSE). ETFs track the performance of a specific index (remember the S&P 500?), sector, or commodity. Unlike a regular stock, where you're investing in only one company, when you purchase an ETF, you're investing in a bunch of different companies in different industry sectors, without having to purchase individual stocks. When you buy an ETF, your investment portfolio is automatically diversified and is tracking some of the best and biggest indexes in the world. Examples: SPDR S&P 500 (SPY), Invesco QQQ Trust (QQQ), Vanguard Total Stock Market ETF (VTI).

Fair Credit Reporting Act (FCRA)—This is a federal law that governs how credit reporting agencies handle your financial information. FCRA determines how consumers' credit information is obtained, how long it is kept, and how it is shared with others. It also limits who is allowed to see your credit report and under what circumstances.

FDIC—Stands for the Federal Deposit Insurance Company. This is a government agency that regulates financial institutions and helps consumers feel confident in placing their money in FDIC-insured banks. As of 2023, FDIC insurance guarantees protection of your funds through $250,000. If you have exposure greater than $250,000 in a bank, you can diversify your funds.

Federal Housing Administration (FHA)—This is a US government agency that ensures loans are approved to borrowers who may not qualify for conventional mortgage loans.

Federal Housing Finance Agency (FHFA)—This is a regulatory government agency that ensures the protection of borrowers and lenders as it relates to the financing housing market. Specifically, they provide regulatory oversight on home loans.

FICO—It stands for the Fair Isaac Corporation. This group created the method we still use today to calculate credit scores. Another pro tip: when someone is referring to their FICO score, they're basically talking about their credit score. These words are often used interchangeably.

financial forecasting—This is a company's crystal ball. The CFO will take the historical performance of the company, factor in the state of the economy and respective industry, and predict the company's financial future.

fixed expenses—Recurring monthly costs like rent, car payment, and utilities. Pretty much all the bills you have to pay but don't always want to.

good debt—Not all debt is bad. More often than not, you will have to take out a loan to add value to your life or increase your net worth. Some examples of good debt include student loans, small-business loans, or a mortgage.

health savings account (HSA)—This is a triple tax-advantaged savings account for employees enrolled in a high-deductible health plan (HDHP). An HSA is designed to help employees and their families save for medical expenses like copays, prescription medicine, and unexpected emergencies.

high-deductible health plan (HDHP)—When your health insurance has a higher deductible than a traditional health plan, making the premium lower.

index fund—A mutual fund or ETF that is designed to mirror the performance of a specific financial market index, like the S&P 500, Russell 2000, or NASDAQ 100.

individual retirement account (IRA)—You know how there's a bunch of different types of candy bars? You've got Hershey's, Snickers, Kit Kat, Butterfinger, Twix, and so on. Well, just like a candy bar, there's a bunch of different types of IRAs that all provide slightly different benefits and offerings. At its core, an IRA is a type of retirement savings account that offers various tax advantages. You can open an IRA at any number of financial institutions including banks, brokerage firms, or mutual fund companies.

insurance premium—This is the amount you pay for insurance every month. This applies to all lines of insurance, like health, auto, home, renters, and life.

liabilities—This is a financial obligation, like a debt or loan that you owe to a financial institution. Some examples are credit cards, auto loans, mortgages, personal loans, or student loans.

liquid assets—If you needed cash fast, what would you do? A liquid asset is anything that you can turn into cash, or liquidate, *fast*. This can be a savings or checking account, money market account, or stock. Anything that takes a while to sell, like a house, is not liquid.

mutual fund—Imagine you and all your friends throw money into a giant pool. That pool of money is then managed by a professional investment company. Math whizzes at the company decide which stocks, bonds, and other securities to invest in, using index funds as a guide. Then the company passes off the earnings back to you, taking a very small percentage for themselves. But it's worth it because the company is doing all the work. Mutual funds can be designed to fit almost any risk profile; ones comprised of primary stocks tend to be riskier, while ones comprised of primary bonds tend to be more conservative. Because there's a significant pool of assets to work with, the company is able to diversify the portfolio and allow you to invest small amounts at a time. But a word of caution, make sure you know what makes up the mutual fund because some may be risky and may carry high expenses!

non-fungible tokens (NFT)—You know how cryptocurrency is like digital money? Well, an NFT is the same, but different. It's similar because an NFT is completely digital. It's different because each NFT is completely unique, both in appearance and value. If I gave you one of my Bitcoins and in return you gave me one of your Bitcoins, we would have traded on a one-for-one basis, and neither of us would have gained or lost anything. Well, unlike Bitcoins, each NFT has its own value and can't really be used to purchase goods or services. They're more collectibles, like digital trading cards. Some NFTs are art or music; others are virtual goods in a video game.

pension plan—This is a unique retirement account offered by employers. While you're an employee, both you and your employer contribute money to the pension plan, which invests it on your behalf. Once you retire, you will receive a monthly pension check, from that retirement fund, to cover your expenses for the rest of your life. It's basically like a recurring retirement paycheck.

personal guarantee—If you're an owner or partner in a new business, the bank will sometimes require you to sign a personal guarantee to secure credit for your company. Essentially, if your business defaults on the loan, you personally are making a legal promise to pay back the debt individually. In the business, people call them a "PG."

profit-sharing plans—This is an additional retirement tool occasionally provided by employers. It's a pretax contribution plan that gives employees a small portion of the company's profits.

rollover IRA—Have you ever switched jobs or are considering doing so in the near future? You may want to consider a rollover IRA. This is when you take your old employer-sponsored retirement account and transfer it to a traditional individual retirement account. Why should you do this? I'm so glad you asked. You'll maintain the tax-deferred status of those retirement savings *and* you'll have more investment options and input over how and where your money is invested. If you're switching jobs, you really need to consider the rollover.

Roth 401(k)—This is similar to the 401(k), but it's a "Roth"—instead of investing using pretax dollars, you're investing post-tax dollars. So, when you withdraw your retirement money later in life, you won't have to worry about paying taxes on that money.

Roth IRA—This account is kind of like the traditional IRA. It's similar in that it's an individual retirement account, but it's different in that it's a "Roth." Instead of investing using pretax dollars, you're investing using post-tax dollars.

S&P 500—Imagine a big basket. The top five hundred companies in the United States are put in this basket, called the S&P 500. And how those five hundred companies perform as a whole is how the fund moves. Every day, analysts conduct research to see which companies should stay in the fund and which companies should be moved out due to performance.

SEP IRA—Stands for Simplified Employee Pension. This retirement account is exclusively used for individuals who are self-employed or small-business owners. Like other employer-sponsored retirement accounts, both the employer and the employee can make contributions.

stocks—Did you ever play with LEGO bricks as a kid? Imagine you built an awesome castle with them. There are thousands of individual LEGO pieces, expertly fit together to create this building. When you purchase stock in a company, you own a tiny, little fraction of the corporation. It's as if you own one LEGO that makes up the castle. The more stocks you buy, the more pieces of the castle you own.

tax lien—When you fail to pay your taxes or debt, the government can lay legal claim to your property.

traditional IRA—This isn't an employer retirement account; it's just run and operated by an individual. This type of retirement savings account is tax deferred. This means the dollars you put into the account are pretax, meaning they haven't been taxed yet. When you make withdrawals from the account, then you will be taxed.

variable expenses—It's variable, it changes! Costs that vary from month to month, like entertainment, shopping, dinners out, or an unexpected car repair.

NOTES

Chapter 2

1. "Relationship Intimacy Being Crushed by Financial Tension: AICPA Survey," American Institute of CPAs, February 4, 2021, https://www .aicpa-cima.com/news/article/relationship-intimacy-being-crushed -by-financial-tension-aicpa-survey.
2. "Relationship Intimacy Being Crushed by Financial Tension: AICPA Survey."
3. "Relationship Intimacy Being Crushed by Financial Tension: AICPA Survey."
4. Jennifer Delgado, "Circles of Trust: Give Everyone the Place They Deserve," Psychology Spot, n.d., https://psychology-spot.com/circle -of-trust-psychology/.
5. "Money Ruining Marriages in America: A Ramsey Solutions Study," Ramsey Solutions, February 6, 2018, https://www.ramseysolutions .com/company/newsroom/releases/money-ruining-marriages-in -america.

Chapter 3

1. "Median Sales Price of Houses Sold for the United States," FRED Economic Data, St. Louis Fed (last accessed August 5, 2023), https:// fred.stlouisfed.org/series/MSPUS.
2. Liz Knueven and Laura Grace Tarpley, "The Average Mortgage Interest Rate by State, Credit Score, Year, and Loan Type," *Business Insider*, August 2, 2023, https://www.businessinsider.com/personal -finance/average-mortgage-interest-rate.
3. "18 U.S. Code § 1029 - Fraud and Related Activity in Connection with Access Devices," Cornell Law School, Legal Information Institute, n.d., https://www.law.cornell.edu/uscode/text/18/1029.
4. Tim Maurer, "Couples: Avoid the Pitfalls of Financial Gaslighting," *Forbes*, May 21, 2021, https://www.forbes.com/sites/timmaurer/2021 /05/29/couples-avoid-the-pitfalls-of-financial-gaslighting/?sh =625ec1df6585.

5. "Financial Infidelity, 2021," NEFE (National Endowment for Financial Education), November 18, 2021, https://www.nefe.org/research/polls /2021/financial-infidelity-2021.aspx.

6. "Credit: What It Is and How It Works," Investopedia, updated February 13, 2023, https://www.investopedia.com/terms/c/credit .asp.

7. Jeff Desjardins, "The History of Consumer Credit in One Giant Infographic," Visual Capitalist, August 29, 2017, https://www.visual capitalist.com/history-consumer-credit-one-infographic/.

8. Jeff Desjardins, "The History of Consumer Credit in One Giant Infographic."

9. "When Were Credit Scores Invented? A Brief Look at History," OppU, updated July 27, 2023, https://www.opploans.com/oppu/articles /a-brief-history-of-credit-scores/.

10. Julia Kagan, "How the Fair Credit Reporting Act (FCRA) Protects Consumer Rights," Investopedia, February 27, 2023, https://www .investopedia.com/terms/f/fair-credit-reporting-act-fcra.asp.

11. Nathan Paulus, "Average Credit Score by Age," MoneyGeek, updated February 26, 2023, https://www.moneygeek.com/credit-cards/analysis /average-credit-score-by-age/.

Chapter 4

1. Jason Fernando, "Balance Sheet: Explanation, Components, and Examples," Investopedia, updated May 4, 2023, https://www .investopedia.com/terms/b/balancesheet.asp#toc-what-is-a-balance -sheet.

2. Carmen Reinicke, "43% of Adults Say They Have Financially Cheated on Their Partner," CNBC, November 18, 2021, https://www.cnbc.com /2021/11/18/43percent-of-adults-say-theyve-cheated-on-their-partner -financially.html.

3. "Money Ruining Marriages in America: A Ramsey Solutions Study."

4. Carmen Reinicke, "43% of Adults Say They Have Financially Cheated on Their Partner."

5. Julia Kagan, "Financial Infidelity: When Couples Lie to Each Other About Money," Investopedia, November 27, 2021, https://www .investopedia.com/terms/f/financial-infidelity.asp.

6. Constance Parten, "Financial Infidelity: Secrets That Destroy Couples," CNBC, March 24, 2011, https://www.cnbc.com/2011/03/24 /Financial-Infidelity:-Secrets-That-Destroy-Couples.html.

7. Matthew Goldberg, "The History of FDIC Insurance Limits," Bankrate, March 24, 2023, https://www.bankrate.com/banking/fdic

-limits-history/#:~:text=Most%20recently%2C%20FDIC%20insurance %20was,deposit%20insurance%20limits%20to%20increase; "Deposit Insurance at a Glance," FDIC (Federal Deposit Insurance Corporation), updated September 13, 2022, https://www.fdic.gov /resources/deposit-insurance/brochures/deposits-at-a-glance/.

8. Cory Mitchell, "Personal Financial Statement: Definition, Uses, and Example," Investopedia, updated October 28, 2020, https://www .investopedia.com/terms/p/personal-financial-statement.asp.

9. Jing Pan, "'Not Living Their Life to Impress Others': These Are the Top Car Brands That Rich Americans Earning More Than $200K Drive Most—Here's Why You Should Steer Toward Them Too," Yahoo!Finance, July 10, 2023, https://finance.yahoo.com/news/not -living-life-impress-others-140000227.html.

Chapter 5

1. Lindsay Bishop, "Average Household Budget: How Much Does the Typical American Spend?" ValuePenguin, November 28, 2022, https:// www.valuepenguin.com/average-household-budget.

2. Karen Bennett, "The Average American Household Budget," Bankrate, September 26, 2023, https://www.bankrate.com/banking/savings /average-household-budget/.

3. Jack Flynn, "20+ Shocking American Savings Statistics [2023]: Average Personal Savings Accounts, Demographics, and Facts," Zippia, February 16, 2023, https://www.zippia.com/advice/american -savings-statistics/.

4. "Gregorian Calendar," Britannica, updated June 20, 2023, https://www .britannica.com/topic/Gregorian-calendar.

5. Mike Brown, "A Study of Seasonal Expenses: Do We Spend More During the Summer?" ElndEDU, May 9, 2023, https://lendedu.com /blog/summer-spending-statistics/.

6. Cheyenne DeVon, "The Average American May Spend Nearly $1,500 on the Holidays," CNBC, December 8, 2022, https://www.cnbc.com /2022/12/08/how-much-americans-may-spend-on-the-holidays .html.

7. Mike Brown, "A Study of Seasonal Expenses."

8. Karen Bennett, "What's the Difference Between Fixed and Variable Expenses?" Bankrate, April 6, 2022, https://www.bankrate.com/banking /fixed-expenses-vs-variable-expenses/.

9. Karen Bennett, "What's the Difference Between Fixed and Variable Expenses?"

10. Bo Davis, "Inflation Takes a Bite at the Restaurant Industry; How Can

Operators Cope?" Modern Restaurant Management, November 21, 2022, https://modernrestaurantmanagement.com/inflation-takes-a-bite-at-the-restaurant-industry-how-can-operators-cope/.

Chapter 6

1. Brandon Vos, "The Right Way to Use Leverage in a Negotiation," Black Swan Group, March 2, 2020, https://www.blackswanltd.com/the-edge/the-right-way-to-use-leverage-in-a-negotiation.
2. Benji Stawski, "8 Ways to Maximize Hilton Honors Redemptions," The Points Guy, February 7, 2022, https://thepointsguy.com/guide/maximizing-redemptions-hilton-honors/.
3. "The Beginner's Guide to Your First Credit Card," Chase, n.d., https://www.chase.com/personal/credit-cards/education/build-credit/how-to-get-your-first-credit-card.
4. American Express Platinum Card homepage, n.d., https://card.americanexpress.com/d/cm/platinum-card/.
5. NFL Extra Points Visa Card homepage, n.d., https://www.nflextrapoints.com/.

Chapter 7

1. Lane Gillespie, "Average American Household Debt Statistics," Bankrate, January 13, 2023, https://www.bankrate.com/personal-finance/debt/average-american-debt/#average-american-household; Ruben Caginalp, "Average Mortgage Debt," Bankrate, October 24, 2022, https://www.bankrate.com/mortgages/average-mortgage-debt/.
2. "Exposure Therapy, Good Therapy," updated July 3, 2015, https://www.goodtherapy.org/learn-about-therapy/types/exposure-therapy.
3. "Credit Card Payoff Calculator, Bankrate, n.d., https://www.bankrate.com/finance/credit-cards/credit-card-payoff-calculator/.
4. Alexandria White, "77% of Americans Are Anxious About Their Financial Situation—Here's How to Take Control," CNBC, updated August 1, 2023, https://www.cnbc.com/select/how-to-take-control-of-your-finances/.
5. "How the Debt Snowball Method Works," Ramsey Solutions, May 3, 2023, https://www.ramseysolutions.com/debt/how-the-debt-snowball-method-works.
6. "Comparing the Snowball and the Avalanche Methods of Paying Down Debt," Wells Fargo, n.d., https://www.wellsfargo.com/goals-credit/smarter-credit/manage-your-debt/snowball-vs-avalanche-paydown/.
7. "What Do I Need to Know About Consolidating My Credit Card

Debt?" CFPB (Consumer Financial Protection Bureau), updated September 23, 2022, https://www.consumerfinance.gov/ask-cfpb/what -do-i-need-to-know-if-im-thinking-about-consolidating-my-credit -card-debt-en-1861/.

8. Matt Schulz, "Average Credit Card Interest Rate in America Today," LendingTree, updated July 17, 2023, https://www.lendingtree.com /credit-cards/average-credit-card-interest-rate-in-america/.

9. "Compare Current Mortgage Rates," NerdWallet, n.d., https://www .nerdwallet.com/mortgages/mortgage-rates.

10. Rae Hartley Beck, "How Is Appreciation Calculated?" Bankrate, June 21, 2022, https://www.bankrate.com/real-estate/home-appreciation /#calculated.

11. "Debt Consolidation Calculator," Bankrate, n.d., https://www.bankrate .com/personal-finance/debt/debt-consolidation-calculator/.

12. Dori Zinn, "What Is Debt Settlement and What Are the Risks?" Bankrate, September 22, 2022, https://www.bankrate.com/personal -finance/debt/what-is-debt-settlement/.

13. "What Is Credit Counseling?" CFPB (Consumer Financial Protection Bureau), updated September 23, 2022, https://www.consumerfinance .gov/ask-cfpb/what-is-credit-counseling-en-1451/.

14. "What Happens When You File for Bankruptcy?" Investopedia, updated July 16, 2023, https://www.investopedia.com/articles/pf/07 /bankruptcy.asp#toc-what-to-do-before-filing-for-bankruptcy.

15. "Calculate Your Debt-to-Income Ratio," Wells Fargo, n.d., https:// www.wellsfargo.com/goals-credit/smarter-credit/credit-101/debt -to-income-ratio/.

16. "What Is a Good Debt-to-Income Ratio?" Wells Fargo, n.d., https:// www.wellsfargo.com/goals-credit/smarter-credit/credit-101/debt -to-income-ratio/understanding-dti/.

17. "What Is Debt-to-Income Ratio—And Why Is It Important?" Bank of America, n.d., https://bettermoneyhabits.bankofamerica.com/en /credit/what-is-debt-to-income-ratio.

Chapter 8

1. Oriana Rosa Royle, "Gen Z Are Leading the Charge on Salary Transparency, but They Would Rather Talk About Their Mental Health and Sex Life Than the State of Their Finances," *Fortune*, February 7, 2023, https://fortune.com/2023/02/07/gen-z-leading -charge-salary-transparency-rather-talk-mental-health-sex-life-than -finances/amp/.

2. "Gen Z Would Rather Talk About Anything but Their Finances,"

BusinessWire, January 31, 2023, https://www.businesswire.com /news/home/20230131005433/en/Gen-Z-Would-Rather-Talk-About -Anything-But-Their-Finances.

3. "Gen Z Would Rather Talk About Anything but Their Finances."

4. "Gen Z Would Rather Talk About Anything but Their Finances."

5. Daniel Hart, "How Athletes Go Bankrupt at an Alarming Rate," American Bankruptcy Institute, January 5, 2018, https://www.abi.org /feed-item/how-athletes-go-bankrupt-at-an-alarming-rate; Siyarri Debbarma, "Despite 65 Percent of NBA Players Going Broke within 5 Years of Retirement, Shaquille O'Neal's Mother Helped Him Buy 175 Restaurants and Amass $450 Million Net Worth," Essentially Sports, September 20, 2022, https://www.essentiallysports.com/nba -basketball-news-despite-65-percent-of-nba-players-going-broke -within-5-years-of-retirement-shaquille-oneals-mother-helped -him-buy-175-restaurants-and-amass-450-million-net-worth/; "What Is the Highest Paid Sport in the World?" WSN, n.d., https://www.wsn. com/blog/highest-paid-sport/.

6. Lane Gillespie, "Average Net Worth Statistics by Age: How Do You Compare?" Bankrate, January 13, 2023, https://www.bankrate.com /personal-finance/average-net-worth-by-age/.

7. Andrew Dunn, "What Is the Average Home Value Increase Per Year?" CreditKarma, August 30, 2022, https://www.creditkarma.com/home -loans/i/average-home-value-increase-per-year.

8. "Median Sales Price of Houses Sold for the United States," FRED Economic Data, St. Louis Fed.

9. Cory Semel, "10 Professions That Require Professional Liability Insurance—Our Guide," SRC, August 27, 2019, https://www .semelriskconsultants.com/10-professions-that-require-professional -liability-insurance-our-guide/.

10. "Be Prepared for a Financial Emergency," FEMA, August 2019, https:// www.ready.gov/sites/default/files/2021-01/ready_financial-emergency _info-sheet.pdf.

11. Holly Johnson, "Term Life Insurance vs. Whole Life Insurance: Which Is Best for You?" CNN Underscored, March 1, 2023, https://www.cnn .com/cnn-underscored/money/term-life-insurance-vs-whole-life.

12. Lisa Smith, "5 Insurance Policies Everyone Should Have," Investopedia, June 25, 2022, https://www.investopedia.com /insurance/insurance-policies-everyone-should-have/.

13. Julia Kagan, "What Is a Postnuptial Agreement? How It Works and What's Included," Investopedia, updated July 14, 2021, https://www .investopedia.com/terms/p/postnuptial_agreement.asp.

14. Bridget Reed Morawski, "What Is a Cohabitation Agreement?" US News and World Report, June 20, 2022, https://money.usnews.com

/money/personal-finance/family-finance/articles/what-is-a
-cohabitation-agreement.

Chapter 9

1. CPI Inflation Calculator, https://www.officialdata.org/canada
   /inflation/1974?endYear=2024&amount=100000&future_pct=0.06.
2. S&P 500 Data, https://www.officialdata.org/us/stocks/s-p-500/1974
   ?amount=100000&endYear=2023.
3. Caitlin O'Kane, "Photo of Connecticut McDonald's $18 Big Mac Meal
   Sparks Debate Online," CBS News, July 20, 2023, https://www
   .cbsnews.com/news/mcdonalds-prices-big-mac-sparks-expensive
   -menu-darien-connecticut-debate-online/.
4. "Inflation Rates in the United States of America," World Data, n.d.,
   https://www.worlddata.info/america/usa/inflation-rates.php#:~:text
   =During%20the%20observation%20period%20from,year%20
   inflation%20rate%20was%204.9%25.
5. "Life Expectancy," World Data, n.d., https://www.worlddata.info/life
   -expectancy.php#:~:text=Life%20expectancy%20for%20men%20
   and,reaching%20an%20age%20of%2080.2.
6. Jeff Grabmeier, "Husbands Still Seen as the Experts on Their
   Household's Finances," Ohio State News, April 12, 2021, https://news
   .osu.edu/husbands-still-seen-as-the-experts-on-their-households
   -finances/.
7. Brendan Porath, "John Daly Citing $55 to $57 Million in Gambling
   Losses Might Mean He's Got It Under Control," SB Nation, May 29,
   2014, https://www.sbnation.com/golf/2014/5/29/5761588/john-daly
   -gambling-addiction-55-million-in-losses.
8. "Stock Market Returns Since 2000," S&P 500 Data, https://www
   .officialdata.org/us/stocks/s-p-500/2000?amount=250000&endYear
   =2023.
9. Gemma Bath, "Forget 50/50. Brené Brown Says the '80/20 Rule' Is the
   Key to a Successful Relationship," MammaMia, February 12, 2020,
   https://www.mamamia.com.au/brene-brown-relationships/.
10. Natasha Knox, "How Can Spouses with Different Risk Tolerances
    Align Their Investments? Think Broader, Says This Planner,"
    Globe and Mail, April 20, 2021, https://www.theglobeandmail
    .com/amp/investing/personal-finance/young-money/article-when-it
    -comes-to-investing-how-can-two-spouses-with-different-risk/.

11. "8 Tips to Align Your Risk Tolerance with Your Spouse's," Regions, n.d., https://www.regions.com/insights/wealth/hervision-herlegacy /your-money/aligning-risk-tolerance-with-your-spouse.

Chapter 10

1. "Guide to Retirement, 2023," JPMorgan Asset Management, n.d., https://am.jpmorgan.com/us/en/asset-management/adv/insights /retirement-insights/guide-to-retirement/.
2. James Chen, "Compounding Interest: Formulas and Examples," Investopedia, updated August 30, 2022, https://www.investopedia .com/terms/c/compounding.asp.
3. Table conducted using this data: https://www.nerdwallet.com /calculator/compound-interest-calculator.
4. "Guide to Retirement, 2023," JPMorgan Asset Management.
5. "Guide to Retirement, 2023," JPMorgan Asset Management.
6. Rob Williams, "Beyond the 4% Rule: How Much Can You Spend in Retirement?" Charles Schwab, February 27, 2023, https://www .schwab.com/learn/story/beyond-4-rule-how-much-can-you-spend -retirement.
7. "Guide to Retirement, 2023," JPMorgan Asset Management.
8. "Be Prepared for a Financial Emergency," FEMA.
9. "Types of Retirement Plans," US Department of Labor, n.d., https:// www.dol.gov/general/topic/retirement/typesofplans.
10. "Types of Retirement Plans," Internal Revenue Service, n.d., https:// www.irs.gov/retirement-plans/plan-sponsor/types-of-retirement -plans.
11. "High Deductible Health Plan (HDHP)," HeathCare.gov, n.d., https:// www.healthcare.gov/glossary/high-deductible-health-plan/.
12. "What Is an HSA?" Morgan Stanley, September 17, 2022, https://www .morganstanley.com/articles/health-savings-account-retirement -tax-advantages#:~:text=HSAs%20are%20savings%20vehicles%20 that,enjoy%20tax%2Dfree%20growth%20potential; "HSA Contribution Limits and Eligibility Rules," Fidelity, July 10, 2023, https://www.fidelity.com/learning-center/smart-money/hsa -contribution-limits.
13. James Royal, "Best IRA Accounts in August 2023," Bankrate, August 1, 2023, https://www.bankrate.com/retirement/best-ira-accounts/.
14. "IRA Contribution Limits for 2022 and 2023," Fidelity, March 2023, https://www.fidelity.com/learning-center/smart-money/ira -contribution-limits.

15. Jake Frankenfield, "Robo-Advisor," Investopedia, updated April 30, 2023, https://www.investopedia.com/terms/r/roboadvisor -roboadviser.asp.

16. Alana Benson, "12 Best Robo-Advisors of August 2023," NerdWallet, August 1, 2023, https://www.nerdwallet.com/best/investing/robo -advisors.

17. "Mutual Funds," Investopedia, n.d., https://www.investopedia.com /mutual-funds-4427787.

18. "Direct Stock Purchase Plan (DSPP)," Corporate Finance Institute, August 18, 2020 (updated January 11, 2023), https://corporatefinance institute.com/resources/equities/direct-stock-purchase-plan-dspp/.

19. "FAQs – Employee Stock Purchase Plans," Fidelity, n.d., https://www .fidelity.com/products/stockoptions/faqpurchase.shtml.

20. Dan Ebinger and Jake Sadler, "Broker vs. Fiduciary: How Are They Different?" Bay Point Wealth, July 18, 2022, https://blog.baypoint wealth.com/broker-vs-fiduciary.

21. "3 Ways an Advisor Can Help Make a Difference," Fidelity, n.d., https://www.fidelity.com/viewpoints/investing-ideas/financial -advisor-cost.

22. "7 Facts About Grocery Shopping That Might Shock You," Five Star Home Foods, July 25, 2017, https://www.fivestarhomefoods.com /blogs/grocery-shopping-facts/.

23. Jason Fernando, "Bond: Financial Meaning with Examples and How They Are Priced," Investopedia, updated March 9, 2023, https://www .investopedia.com/terms/b/bond.asp.

24. James Royal, "Best Index Funds in August 2023," Bankrate, August 1, 2023, https://www.bankrate.com/investing/best-index-funds /#more-top.

The Closing Bell

1. Kelly Jensen, "Over 50% of Adults Have Not Finished a Book in the Last Year," Book Riot, June 21, 2022, https://bookriot.com/american -reading-habits-2022/.

INDEX

ABOUT THE AUTHOR

JASON TARTICK is a *Wall Street Journal* best-selling author, the host of Apple's chart-topping business podcast *Trading Secrets*, cofounder of Rewired Talent Management (RTM), entrepreneur, investor, and speaker. Jason worked for nearly ten years in banking, earned his MBA in accounting and finance, and executed more than $150 million in lending transactions before taking a career detour into reality television. He is most known from his time spent as a contestant on ABC's *The Bachelorette*.

Special Acknowledgment: Natalie Thompson Creps

Natalie, we did it! As you know, it was recommended to me by the "pros" in this world to ensure I hired a cowriter with an extensive résumé, experience, and recognition through their past writings. Some of the best decisions I've ever made in my life involved going against the majority. Taking a chance and hiring an applicant from the internet who had a burning passion to enter this space was the best decision I made for Book 2. From a stranger online to a colleague to a lifelong friend—thank you for the consistency, resilience, adaptability, and execution. It was flawless. I couldn't have done it without you. Thanks again for everything, Natalie!

—Jason Tartick